HAUNTED HOUSES

D0187430

Edrick Thay

GHOST
HOUSE

Ghost House Books

The Publisher: Ghost House Books
Distributed by Lone Pine Publishing

10145 – 81 Avenue   1808-B Street NW, Suite 140
Edmonton, AB T6E 1W9   Auburn, WA
Canada   USA 98001

Website: http://www.ghostbooks.net

National Library of Canada Cataloguing in Publication Data
Thay, Edrick, 1977–

 Haunted houses / Edrick Thay.

 ISBN 1–894877–30–6

 1. Haunted houses. I. Title.

BF1475.T42 2003   133.1'22   C2002–911491–8

Editorial Director: Nancy Foulds
Project Editor: C.D. Wangler
Illustrations Coordinator: Carol Woo
Production Manager: Gene Longson
Cover Design: Gerry Dotto
Layout & Production: Jeff Fedorkiw

Photo Credits: Every effort has been made to accurately credit photographers. Any errors or omissions should be directed to the publisher for changes in future editions. The photographs in this book are reproduced with the kind permission of the following sources: Chicago Historical Society (p. 13), J. Robert Salts (p. 29), Columbus Historic Foundation (p. 61), National Archives, Still Pictures Branch (p. 107: NWDNS-111-B-3396); Cranston Historical Society (p. 109: Lydia Rapazo); Nottingham Castle Museum and Gallery (p. 91, 121, 124, 125); Nova Scotia Archives and Records Management (p. 129); National Archives of Canada (p. 171: PA-134127); Toronto Public Library (p. 178: S-1-1138); Virginia Department of Historic Resources (p. 183); New Orleans Public Library (p. 218); North Carolina Department of Cultural Resources (p. 249: Elizabeth Faison); Library of Congress (p. 51: HABS,VA,7-ALEX,17-7; p. 54: HABS,VA,7-ALEX,17-10; p. 74: D43-T01-1792; p. 79, 131: USZ62-25793; p. 82, USZ62-103900; p. 97: HABS,MO,97-SAIGEN,9-22; p. 99: HABS,MO,97-SAIGEN,9-23; p. 134: HABS,KY,37-FRAFO,2-1; p. 137: HABS,KY,37-FRAFO,28; p. 144: USW3-20494-D; p. 148: USZ62-104639; p. 151: HABS,CAL,27-MONT,18-6; p. 157: USZ62-78468; p. 160: HABS,TEX,84-GALV,1-4; p. 168, 173: USZ62-097458; p. 175: USZ62-093719; p. 188: HABS,DC,WASH,134-4; p. 190: USZ62-111451; p. 198: HABS,CAL,37-OLTO,5-2; p. 48, 200: HABS,CAL,37-OLTO,5-7; p. 210: HABS,DEL,1-DOV,6-1; p. 213: HABS, DEL,1-DOV,6-4; p. 10, 224: HABS,MASS,8-HAD,7-2; p. 229: HABS,SC,10-CHAR,246-2; p. 215, 236: HABS,NJ,16-RING,1-1; p. 242: USZ62-16475; p. 244: HABS,DEL,1-DOV.V,1-2).

The stories, folklore and legends in this book are based on the author's collection of sources including individuals whose experiences have led them to believe they have encountered phenomena of some kind or another. They are meant to entertain, and neither the publisher nor the author claims these stories represent fact.

We acknowledge the financial support of the Government of Canada through the Book Publishing Industry Development Program (BPIDP) for our publishing activities.

PC: P6

To Natalie Dalton
Thanks for the tip.

CONTENTS

Chapter Four: Lady of the House

Chapter Five: Infamous Abodes

Chapter Six: Colonial Estates

Acknowledgments

There are many people to thank and I wish I had room to thank them all. Dedicated researcher Alana Bevan compiled the information for most of these stories, sifting through numerous sources to find the most interesting and human accounts. Without her critical eye, I would have had nothing of substance to write. Many thanks, Alana. The office isn't the same without you. Has Billy Tauzin responded yet?

For guidance, Alana followed those who had gone before her; it is to these individuals I am indebted as well. Dennis William Hauck's *International Directory of Haunted Places* proved a most valuable resource; Mr. Hauck has my thanks for helping to simplify a daunting task. The Southwest Virginia Ghosthunters Society has researched sites along the Atlantic coast, and its narratives concerning houses such as the Guibourd-Valle House and the Castle Hill Mansion were beautifully and richly rendered, setting an example for what I hoped to achieve in this collection. For its precision, dedication and care, the society has my deepest gratitude. Also unwavering in its devotion to uncovering stories that fall on the periphery, is the website hauntedhouses.com, an informative and lively stop for information concerning virtually any haunted house in the United States. A high standard has been set not just by these individuals, but also those others who dedicate their lives to exploring the world of shadows. I can only hope I do these stories justice.

I also owe thanks to the staff at Ghost House Books. Carol Woo has once again managed to find the photos and images that imbue this book with an immediacy and intimacy that my words fail to convey alone. You have the sincerest of thanks from Chief Plenty Coups, Carol. Many thanks also to Chris Wangler, who, in addition to editing my text into the work you hold in your hands now, took time from a busy schedule to research stories for me so I could concentrate on the book's writing. This book is as much his as it is mine. Dan Asfar also deserves a hearty pat on the back for keeping me sane on those days when the words eluded me and when I wanted nothing more than to throw my keyboard into my computer monitor. Thanks for the push, Big Dan Montana.

And finally, there are not words enough to express my appreciation to both Nancy Foulds and Shane Kennedy for giving me this opportunity to indulge my love for writing a good story. Because of them, I am doing that most glorious of things—I am writing. I must thank them for their faith in my abilities and for their compassion.

Introduction

We tend to think of our homes as secure, private places—sanctuaries from a world that threatens to overwhelm us with its attendant stresses. Yet rarely do we consider that in the daily comings and goings of our lives we might be intruders in the lives of spirits who have never moved away. Every house, after all, is as much a reflection of its past as its present. And as the stories in this book illustrate, every now and then a house's past will reveal itself in quite unexpected ways.

Although many of the ghosts in this collection led lives very different from our own, many are no different from you or me. These lingering spirits were once living breathing beings, and it's comforting to think that in death they retain the same longings and desires that motivated them in life.

How else can one explain why some houses are haunted? Spirits love their houses as we do. At home we are able to relax, strip away the facades and be our most comfortable self. For spirits seeking a place to feel secure, their former homes provide an ideal setting.

Of course, the living are not always eager to share a space with spirits. After all, although we are born equal, we are not created equal. In this book there are terrifying accounts of cruelty and selfishness beyond belief. In some cases, it is the perpetrators who overstay their welcome. Little wonder, then, that decent human beings might choose not to live in the DeFeo House in Amityville, New York, or Lalaurie House in New Orleans, Louisiana. The spirits in these places are of a special ilk—symbols of an evil that never sleeps. But, as with all things, one must be careful not to paint all the hauntings with the same brush. There are plenty of accounts in which the living are more than willing to share their homes with ghosts because those spirits embody a special dignity.

Take Jules Valle, who was visited by three Spanish apparitions that eased his recovery while he was recuperating from eye surgery in the Guibourd House in Ste. Genevieve, Missouri. The ghosts were goodwill personified, and Valle spent another happy decade in the house, ever mindful of what the spirits had done for him. Indeed, for the most part, the living and the dead exist quite peacefully.

But this is not the popular belief. Most people think a haunted house squats glumly on a hill, gaping in the moonlight like some maw of death, populated with specters bent on frightening visitors and residents. Such a picture denies ghosts their humanity. Death does not render them any less human, and for the most part these spirits are achingly vulnerable, like Bettie Brown of Ashton Villa in Galveston, Texas, and Amasa Sprague of the Sprague Mansion in Rhode Island. To learn their histories and to respect them is to catch a glimpse of ourselves.

Take from these stories what you will. I hope they prove entertaining and educational. Consider that even in our homes we remain a part of the world at large, and that we should never be so arrogant or bold to think that we stand outside a house's history. I hope you catch a glimpse of the marvelous in humanity—of both the uniqueness and the sameness of human existence.

1
Devil's Dens

Although most spirits in haunted houses pose little threat to the living, some vengeful poltergeists and angry specters are defined by their cruelty. Not even death can stay their evil intentions. Unfortunately, skeptics often attribute their fantastic stories to a longing for fame on the part of the storytellers. Regardless, nothing discounts the evil done within these homes, either by residents or by outsiders. If not haunted by ghosts, then these houses are surely haunted by their pasts.

Hull House
CHICAGO, ILLINOIS

In 1912, a man came to the corner of Polk and Halsted, carrying in his arms what appeared to be a baby wrapped in a blanket. But this child was far from ordinary. Its ears were pointed and its skin was scaly. If not for the blanket, the child's tail and hoofed feet would certainly have attracted attention. As it happened, nobody thought anything unusual, and the man approached Hull House without arousing curiosity. He knocked at the door three times and waited impatiently for Jane Addams to answer.

Jane Addams was the operator of Hull House, a settlement house in the slums of Chicago's Near West Side. Addams had graduated from Rockford College in 1882, but was restless and unsure about the future. The idea of settling down into a life of homemaking and limited social participation didn't appeal to her; instead, she traveled through Europe where she had an unexpected epiphany.

While in London, Addams visited Toynbee Hall in the Whitechapel district. It was the first time she had seen a settlement house and what she saw was inspiring: the educated middle-class living among the working class and the poor, helping to organize clubs, recreation and education. What truly impressed Addams was that these people were not professional social workers or welfare agents. They were simply individuals who would no longer rely on an often indifferent government to cure society's ills; they would right the wrongs themselves. For Addams, the experience was pivotal. She returned to Chicago.

Witnesses have seen a mysterious child's face in the left attic window of Hull House in Chicago.

Chicago's identity is defined by its position between the factories and plants of the Northeast and the fields and farms of the Midwest. As America continued its westward expansion, industries involved in transportation, manufacturing and commerce prospered, fueling the need for cheap labor. The federal government sought out immigrants from Europe to fill the need, and they arrived in droves.

Most immigrants arrived with nothing more than their dreams and the clothes on their backs. Desperate for work, they were easily exploited by employers who were unwilling to pay decent wages. Unable to afford any other housing, the workers congregated in overcrowded tenements, creating the urban slum. In Chicago, these workers lived in the west side, where overcrowding, insufficient sanitation and general neglect led to rampant crime and disease. Public welfare agencies were ill-equipped to deal with the problem. Addams saw an opportunity to make a difference.

In 1856, Charles J. Hull built the house that still bears his name to use as a country estate. By the time Jane Addams first saw the property some 30 years later, the countryside that had lured Hull from the city had been replaced by the factories and tenement houses of the urban slum. But Addams found exactly what she sought in the building. In 1889, she was granted a 25-year, rent-free lease. Hull House opened later that year to aid the indigent and their children. Originally a kindergarten, the center expanded to include a nursery and a care center and began to offer adults college-level classes. The complex was later enhanced with the addition of a gymnasium, shops, playgrounds and housing for children. Addams would go on to win a Nobel Prize for her social work in 1931, so it's not surprising that when the man was thinking of places to take his odd baby, Hull House was one of the first places to come to mind. He wanted to be rid of his curse as soon as possible.

The man's story began when a Catholic woman and her atheist husband learned of her pregnancy. According to legend, the wife attempted to hang a picture of the Virgin Mary in the home upon hearing the news, but the husband refused, claiming that he would rather see the Devil himself than hang such a picture in his home. Somebody took the man at his word, because when his child was born, something was quite clearly wrong. Soon enough, the man found himself walking to the corner of Halsted and Polk to prevail upon Addams' generosity.

When Addams answered the door, the man begged her to take his child and raise it. Addams agreed and the child was left in her care. Physical oddities aside, it became obvious that the child might very well be Satan's spawn. When Addams attempted to baptize it, it shrieked and crawled away, cackling. Since it resisted all attempts at forging relationships, Addams was left with no choice but to lock the increasingly combative and aggressive child in the attic.

With so many workers passing in and out of Hull House, it wasn't long before the neighborhood locals were entertaining each other with stories of the devil child at Hull House. The property found itself inundated with people hoping to catch a glimpse of its notorious ward. Addams refused to acknowledge the child's existence, turning away the curious. Few believed Addams' denials, especially when people claimed that they had seen the wild child peering out at the world from behind an attic window. Years passed and before long some began to doubt that the devil child ever existed. Those who believe the story felt Addams was only protecting the child and that was why he was guarded so zealously. His existence is supported by the fact that his spirit still haunts Hull House.

Those passing by Hull House will sometimes see the ghostly image of a deformed child's face in the left attic window. It peers down to the street below, in the same way as the devil baby did so many years ago, inspiring fear and dread in those who see it. In fact, the story was the inspiration for the book and film *Rosemary's Baby*. But the devil baby is not the only spirit to still call Hull House home.

Even while Jane Addams lived in the home, she was constantly disturbed from sleep by loud footsteps in her bedroom. Yet when she looked around her room, it was empty. Addams eventually moved to another room to find peace. Other guests who stayed in the same bedroom said their sleep was interrupted by strange and eerie sounds. It was later revealed that Charles J. Hull's wife died in the second-floor bedroom of natural causes and continued to roam the room long after her death. One evening, a guest awoke to see a figure in the darkness standing near the bed. She lit the gas lamp, but the light only revealed how empty the room was. A feeling of sadness is said to permeate the room, but it seems as if Mrs. Hull means no harm. Like many other ghosts in haunted houses, she is merely unwilling to leave her home.

Summerwind
LAND O' LAKES, WISCONSIN

Arnold Hinshaw had a problem. Workers he had hired to renovate his new house were refusing to come to work. Every day it seemed as if they had a new excuse, ranging from exhaustion to other contracts. Hinshaw quickly concluded that he would have to do the work himself. His workers' reluctance to work only emphasized what he already knew all too well—the dream home he'd bought for his young family was more a hell than a paradise.

Hinshaw and his wife, Ginger, brought their six children to Land o' Lakes, Wisconsin. Their new home had been built in 1916 by Robert P. Lamont to serve as his summer home. Lamont served as Secretary of Commerce under President Herbert Hoover, so he wanted an idyllic retreat from the pressures and stress of Washington, D.C. Perhaps if Hinshaw had heard the stories about what had happened to Lamont while he lived in the home, he could have avoided the greatest upheaval in his life.

From the time it was built, Summerwind had a reputation for being haunted. The account repeated with the most frequency details how Lamont was awakened one night by the sounds of an intruder moving around his kitchen. He crept out of his bedroom, pausing only to draw his pistol, then walked down the stairs. In the dim moonlight coming through the kitchen window, Lamont saw a shadowy figure moving in front of the basement door. He didn't hesitate, firing two shots at the form. His aim was true.

But no body fell to the ground. There were no cries of pain or agony. And when Lamont walked over to the basement door, he saw why. There was nobody there. He had fired two shots into the door. Lamont was stunned. So what had he fired at? What had he seen lurking in the darkness? What had he heard scrounging around his kitchen so loudly that he was roused from slumber by the sound? Lamont never did determine what exactly happened that night, but when he died, it seemed that whatever spirit had been in the house departed too. A succession of owners came and went but it wasn't until the Hinshaws arrived in the 1970s that things began to get a little strange. Although the Hinshaws lived there for only half a year, in hindsight it was probably six months too long.

From the moment they moved in, the Hinshaws were plagued by menacing voices, threatening shadows and unusual shapes. Walking by a bedroom, the Hinshaw children heard a whisper that persisted until they entered the room. Vague figures walked the hallways and the ghost of a woman floated again and again in front of the French doors that opened into the parlor. And then there was the recurring opening and closing of windows and doors throughout the house. One window so insistently refused to stay shut that Hinshaw was forced to hammer it closed with a nail. The refrigerator in the kitchen would stop running, only to start again just minutes before a repairman was scheduled to arrive. The same thing happened with other appliances, such as the dishwasher and the deep freezer. In one bizarre incident, Hinshaw's vehicle burst into flames just as he was about to unlock the car door. Hinshaw called the local fire department, but investigators never found an earthly cause for the blaze.

Despite its idyllic name, Summerwind was a house possessed. The renovators Hinshaw had hired finally told him that they wanted nothing more to do with the job. The Hinshaws would have to do the job themselves. Their decision proved to be the beginning of the end.

Hinshaw was painting the inside of a bedroom closet. One of the walls was taken up with a large shoe drawer. Hinshaw moved the unit from the wall to reveal a hidden area, large and dark, musty with age. He peered into the darkness, wondering what might have been stored inside the space. He switched on his flashlight and shone its beam across the space when something caught his eye. In the weak light, Hinshaw couldn't be sure what he was looking at, but it looked like it could be the body of a small animal. He called for one of his daughters.

With flashlight in hand, his daughter crawled in and then tore the air with a horrifying scream. Hinshaw called after his child, pleading with her to come out. She did and what she bore in her hand chilled Hinshaw's blood. Hinshaw found himself staring at a skull; it was clear that the body in the space was the remains of a human being. It was never explained why, but the Hinshaws never contacted the authorities about their find. Perhaps they decided that it was best to let the past die. The shoe drawer was put back in place, and the corpse stayed where it had been found. But something evil had been awakened when that corpse was disturbed and it began to work its way into Hinshaw's mind, driving the man to the very edge of reason.

During times of stress, Hinshaw often found relief by playing his Hammond organ. Not long after the discovery of the body, he began to play the organ as if possessed. Tunes that had once been recognizable and comforting now became strange and frenzied, as if the melodies were inspired not by the divine, but by the devilish. Hinshaw would hammer at the organ throughout the night; his family, unable to sleep, huddled in the master bedroom together, terrified and confused by everything happening around them. Hinshaw's wife begged him to stop frightening his family, but he refused, claiming that demons possessed him and compelled him to play their music. Soon enough, no one could decipher exactly what it was that Hinshaw said or did. The alleged voices had taken over for good; as a result, his distraught wife attempted suicide.

Hinshaw was sent to a hospital for treatment, while his wife and their children headed north to Granton, Wisconsin, where Mrs. Hinshaw's parents lived. There, Mrs. Hinshaw suffered as she watched her husband descend further into madness, transformed into a man she barely recognized. She divorced him and married another.

She hadn't been married long before her father, Raymond Bober, announced that he was going to buy Summerwind. He had plans, he said, to transform the house into a restaurant and inn. Its success was all but assured by its scenic location along the lakefront. His daughter, of course, protested and begged him to leave the house alone. When pressed for details about her reluctance, she remained silent; her father, for his part, remained undeterred. He went ahead and bought the home before bringing his family down to help him renovate.

Only then did the former Mrs. Hinshaw mention to her father and her new husband that they had found a body in the bedroom closet, that the home was haunted, and that it had driven her former husband insane. Bober was not surprised.

He claimed that he had bought Summerwind partly because he had been inspired by the spirit of explorer John Carver who had visited Bober in a dream. Carver, Bober believed, had been granted the northern third of Wisconsin by the Sioux when he had negotiated a peace between two warring tribes. The deed was said to be in a black box under the foundations of Summerwind. Bober claimed that Carver still haunted the house, caught in an endless search for the deed.

Bober's new son-in-law was aghast at the idea of a corpse in the closet, and despite his wife's protests, he raced to the closet and threw back the shoe drawer. A smaller man than Hinshaw, he managed to crawl into the space only to find nothing there. His wife was shocked. Where had the body gone? Had she imagined the whole thing? She couldn't know for certain anymore. Bober, on the other hand, seemed far more concerned with getting the renovations underway than looking after his daughter. But as with Arnold Hinshaw, renovation efforts proved frustrating.

Workers were always losing their tools and felt as if they were under constant surveillance. Their problems were only exacerbated by the house's peculiar ability to expand and shrink. Measurements taken one day in one room would be wrong the next. Work was next to impossible. And then came the day when Bober's son, Karl, was working alone in the house. Rain began to fall, so Karl went through the house, closing all the windows. While upstairs, he heard someone calling out for him. Karl didn't know what to think about the voice, but he knew that he was supposed to be alone. He began searching the house to see if anyone was there, but found nobody. When he reached the front room, he heard two shots fired from a gun in the kitchen. Karl raced to the room. The air was thick with smoke and gunpowder. When it cleared, Karl found himself staring at an empty room. All the doors in the house were still locked, all the windows securely fastened. Plans for Raymond Bober's restaurant and inn were put on hold indefinitely.

Summerwind is no more. Three investors bought the home in 1986 after it had been abandoned for years, with plans to restore the 20-room mansion to its previous splendor. But just two years later, during a thunderstorm, lightning struck the house and it burned to the ground. No deed promising John Carver the northern third of Wisconsin was ever found. No explanation for the discovery and subsequent disappearance of the corpse was ever offered. Doubt persists as to whether or not the events that Bober eventually wrote about in a book, *The Carver Effect*, actually ever happened. Skeptics believe he was only trying to promote his business venture with the paranormal tales. But if that was the case, then why weren't the renovations ever completed? Why did two attempts to restore the home fail so miserably? Unfortunately, the mystery of Summerwind may remain forever unsolved.

The Donnelly Homestead
BIDDULPH TOWNSHIP, ONTARIO

It is a place where animals fear to tread, a land blotted by the stain of a crime committed years ago. On a winter night in 1880, a mob of men, led by Constable James Carroll, broke into James Donnelly's farmhouse. They entered Donnelly's bedroom, where, with a series of blows to the head with a club, the mob dropped the Irish immigrant to the floor. They then plunged a pitchfork into his back, the tines puncturing various parts of Donnelly's anatomy. He was left for dead. His wife, Johannah, was pummeled senseless in the kitchen, and the family dog was killed. Bridget, a cousin sleeping over that night, was murdered. Two of the Donnelly children were subdued and then died when the mob turned the family homestead into a funeral pyre.

Constable James Carroll and five others were arrested for their actions that night, but a trial failed to produce a conviction—one of the more puzzling aspects of a story that has fascinated Canadians for over a century. How were so many allowed to go unpunished for the crime? Some claimed it was justified, that the Donnellys deserved their fates. Others disputed the point. All agreed that Biddulph Township did not escape unscathed from the murders. The Donnelly Homestead became haunted—a place animals curiously avoid as the anniversary of the massacre approaches. But while some animals have mysteriously died around the property, the Donnelly spirits have been surprisingly accommodating to humans. Far from vengeful, they seem no different than spirits who wake the living with phantom footsteps or assert their presence with taps on the shoulder. They do serve, however, as grim reminders of the darkness lurking within us all.

James and Johannah Donnelly arrived in Ontario in the early 1840s and settled in Forest City, now known as London. Son William was born a short time later. Life in Forest City was far from idyllic. Although its name suggested a harmonious blend of both rural and urban, the Donnellys found the city lacking in the former. They wanted to feel the ground beneath their feet, to smell the earth between their fingers and to watch the sun and rain give life to their dreams. They decided to move to the country to escape the many pressures of city life.

The only problem—and it was a big one—was that the Donnellys lacked the necessary means to secure land for a farm. So they squatted. They arrived in Biddulph Township and claimed 100 acres of land from an absentee landlord, John Grace. For a few years, life for the Donnellys was a dream realized; everything that they had envisioned came to pass. In addition to William, five more children were born to James and Johannah: four boys and, finally, a girl named Jennie—enough hands to ensure the continued prosperity of the family farm. They wanted for nothing, finding in each other and the land everything they needed.

Patrick Farrell's dreams were similar to the Donnellys'. He too wanted land so he could begin a farm, but one crucial difference was that Farrell was willing to obtain his land legally. In 1855, John Grace had sold 50 acres of his land to Michael Maher who, in turn, offered the land to Farrell to rent. Blissfully unaware of the arrangement, James Donnelly was startled one day to see a stranger moving onto what he believed to be his property. Donnelly was incensed; he had worked too hard on the land to see it taken away from him. Pitchfork in hand, he chased a surprised and frightened Farrell off the land.

Farrell collected himself and thought about the situation. There was no reason he should be chased off his land. He had paid Maher good money for the right to use the property. The crazed fellow with the pitchfork was undoubtedly a squatter. If anyone should be wielding an instrument of death, it should be Farrell. Farrell took the case to court where a judge decided that Donnelly could keep half the land, but would have to relinquish the rest to Farrell. The decision sat poorly with James, but he managed to keep calm, at least for a short while. Bolstered by alcohol at a logging bee, James gave full vent to his rage when he ran into a similarly drunken and enraged Farrell. They first exchanged words and then blows. Within moments, Farrell was dead. Using a concealed handspike, James had stabbed his nemesis in the head.

A warrant was issued for James' arrest, but he disappeared. Repeated searches of the Donnelly homestead turned up nothing; if family members knew where James was, they refused to enlighten the authorities. Watchful neighbors reported that the murderer was hiding in his fields and would make an occasional appearance beside his wife, disguised in a woman's clothing. He knew the fields better than anyone, though, and try as they might, neither the authorities nor local vigilantes could ever find him.

James passed the summer and fall months in his fields, but once winter arrived his situation became dire. It was far too cold and he'd die before spring returned to revive the land. With no options, James turned himself in. His death sentence was commuted to seven years in Kingston Penitentiary, thanks to the hard work of his wife, who petitioned to have the sentence overturned.

While life in prison must have been difficult for James, life outside was not any easier for the family he left behind. As the relations of a convicted killer, the Donnellys were shunned by the community. James' sins had infected his brood. The children were bullied and teased without mercy, the torment creating hardened hearts and crueler constitutions. As the years passed, the Donnelly children, ever mindful of the past, became the aggressors, meting out vitriol and punishment to those who had once been their judges. The Donnellys were fast becoming the scourge of Biddulph Township.

James' release in 1862 elicited vicious responses from the community. The Donnellys' continued presence in Biddulph Township threatened the peace and security of a law-abiding, God-fearing society. The Donnellys were a disease, a malignancy whose spread had to be stopped. A rash of barn burnings, animal mutilations, beatings and other crimes were blamed on the family. To protect themselves, the people created the Property Protection Association, an organization dedicated to rooting out criminal elements—as long as the perpetrators were Donnellys.

When a barn burned down, the Property Protection Association seized the opportunity. No matter what, the Donnellys would have to shoulder the blame. First, they accused the Donnelly boys of the crime, but a plausible alibi prevented the charges from sticking. Then the blame was shifted to the parents. A trial date was set. As the date approached, it became clear that a trial would only prove the

Donnellys' innocence. No evidence could be found linking them to the crime.

If the law would not provide the locals with satisfaction, then the Property Protection Association was ready to resort to vigilante justice. They decided to beat confessions out of the Donnellys. On the night of February 3, 1862, 35 men, led by Constable James Carroll, arrived at the Donnelly farm. Within hours, most of the Donnellys were dead and their home had been set ablaze.

The citizens tried to forget about the crime, unwilling to face the consequences of their actions or to deal with their own debasement. But the spirits haunting the homestead are a constant reminder of what took place that winter night.

The old Roman Line Road runs near the Donnelly property. As the anniversary of the massacre approaches, animals, notably horses, begin behaving strangely while passing through the area. They will come to a complete stop, refusing to move any further. If forced to do so, they become erratic, crazed. Some horses have actually died after passing through the area on February 4.

Those living on the Donnelly homestead have reported strange phenomena for years. One couple, having heard the eerie stories, was allowed to pass the evening in the barn. They were awakened during the night by approaching footsteps. Then the man felt pressure on his chest, as if someone was standing on him. Most puzzling of all was that the barn, save for the couple, was empty. Two students exploring the barn felt the same sensation, while one reported that she heard screams in her head. One of the home's owners was taking a shower once and saw the shadow of something or someone entering the bathroom. Yet when he pulled back the curtain to see who was there, he saw only an empty room.

Others have seen ghosts—images of a man and woman clad in black and two children clad in white. A psychic brought into the home by the A&E television network sensed the presence of a young woman believed to be Jennie Donnelly, James and Johannah's only daughter. James and Johannah are thought to survive in the ghosts of a tall, mustached man, accompanied by a woman with her hair pulled back into a bun. People working in the kitchen are often overwhelmed by depression and have heard their names called out. Visitors and residents both feel that they're being watched from the moment they enter the house. Those passing through the area have also felt that something is not quite right.

In 1976, a group of teenagers parked their car at St. Patrick's Cemetery at night, putting to the test the rumors they'd heard from so many others. They hadn't been waiting long when they were treated to a light show few have ever had the opportunity to witness. On the Roman Line Road, blue bolts of lightning were arcing up and down the street. Back and forth they went, brilliant crackling waves of electricity.

Spooked, the teenagers raced out of the car and into the cemetery. There, they saw a black silhouetted figure rising from a grave. The vision was enough to scare them away from the site, never to return. Coincidentally, the Donnellys had been buried in St. Patrick's Cemetery. In 1994, a man with a camcorder visited the site and recorded the Donnelly tombstone. When he watched the tape later, a shadow he hadn't seen that day mysteriously appeared next to the tombstone. It was there one moment and gone the next.

The Donnelly family tombstone, erected in 1964. It replaced the original, erected in 1889.

Photographs taken in and around the site often show an unexplained mist fogging up the images. While some believe the mist is nothing more than vapor from exhaling on a cold winter's day, others insist it is proof of the paranormal presence of the Donnellys.

Why the people of Biddulph Township were allowed to execute the Donnelly family has never been explained. Eager to stamp out a perceived threat to their traditional lifestyle, they became the evil that they feared. Whether or not they relished the irony or even recognized it has been lost to the past. All that remains is an area haunted by sin and death.

Lalaurie Mansion
NEW ORLEANS, LOUISIANA

In New Orleans, there is a mansion whose stately exterior barely hints at the terror and torture that took place within its walls so many years ago. As it is with so much in life, things are rarely what they seem. Those familiar with the home's gruesome history scurry past the house at 1140 Royal Street, mostly because lingering on the sidewalk may force them to confront the evils that lurk within the hearts of even the best men. Listen closely and these locals can be heard uttering four words, as if attempting to ward off danger. "La maison est hantée," they whisper. "La maison est hantée." Translated, these words mean the house is haunted. The house they refer to is the opulent and grand Lalaurie Mansion, a private residence populated with specters that will spend eternities scarred and confused because a woman was unable to resist the demons of her soul.

There was a time when, to be a part of the New Orleans elite, one had to be invited to the Lalaurie Mansion. To cross the home's threshold was to enter a world of privilege, status and class. It was to know the favor of Madame Delphine Macarty Lalaurie, the most influential French-Creole woman in the city, a position fortified with great wealth and prominence. Those fortunate enough to grace her presence believed Lalaurie to be a caring and attentive woman who could speak knowledgeably on almost every topic. She was charismatic, charming and radiant.

She moved into 1140 Royal Street in 1832 and spared no expense in acquiring the finest furnishings and possessions.

Doors were made of imported mahogany and hand-carved by carpenters. Chandeliers, each with hundreds of candles, lit up each room. Tending to each and every detail of the home was Lalaurie's small army of slaves, a band so numerous that Lalaurie's guests often remarked that she must have had a slave for every conceivable task.

To her guests, Lalaurie must have appeared as the most demanding of mistresses. Some never noticed, but others found the frequency with which Lalaurie replaced her slaves somewhat puzzling, even in a city where slaves were constantly sold for profit or set free. She changed them as often as most people changed their shirts. Slaves rarely served parties twice and very few of them seemed capable of meeting Lalaurie's obviously high standards. Or so it seemed. The truth was as horrifying as the house was opulent.

Pedestrians in the French Quarter were stunned one afternoon as they walked by 1140 Royal Street. They couldn't help recoiling with fear when they heard the desperate cries of a girl from above. Looking up to the mansion's rooftop, they saw one of Lalaurie's slaves screaming for help, her face a study in pure terror. Her clothes were torn and blood flowed from the cuts that marked her back and arms. She raced across the rooftop as if pursued.

Madame Lalaurie herself then appeared, whip in hand. Before a crowd that could only stare aghast, she began to flog the girl. The air filled with the crack of the whip meeting flesh and agonized shrieks that cleaved the heart. Lalaurie was fury unleashed, the poor slave girl its focus. Who knows what ran through the poor girl's mind, but she must have known that death was at hand. But if she was going to die, it would be on her terms and not those of her crazed mistress.

With the last of her ebbing strength, the girl raised herself to her feet, to the amazement of the disbelieving crowd, and leapt from the building into the gated courtyard.

The authorities were summoned and soon policemen were swarming Lalaurie's mansion, looking for the slave girl. Their search didn't last long. In the yard, underneath a stand of cypress trees, officers found freshly dug dirt. In that shallow grave was the dead body of the servant girl that Lalaurie had flogged to death. But because slaves were seen as property rather than people, Lalaurie was not sentenced to a term in prison, but was fined and forced to sell her slaves at a public auction instead. The fine she easily absorbed and at the auction Lalaurie had relatives and friends buy her slaves and then return them to her in secret. But while Lalaurie might have escaped with little punishment, the damage to her reputation was done and it proved most corrosive. Word spread throughout New Orleans about the vindictive and cruel Delphine Macarty Lalaurie. As it did, more and more families and individuals refused to be tainted with her stench.

Within months, the chandeliers at 1140 Royal Street that once shone down upon hordes of socialites now cast their light upon empty rooms, the harsh glare off the polished hardwood floors underscoring the mansion's emptiness. Once adored and revered, the Lalaurie name was now shunned and avoided; it had become a disease to those who once courted it, although few could have suspected exactly how great Lalaurie's depravity was. That much became all too clear one spring evening in 1834.

A fire broke out in the kitchen of the Lalaurie Mansion. When the fire brigade responded to the call, they found Lalaurie's cook chained to the kitchen floor. The elderly black woman who claimed to have set the fire because death in a pyre was preferable to the punishment and abuse to which she had been subjected each and every day in Lalaurie's service. The flames were extinguished, but before the fire brigade could leave, the cook begged the men to go upstairs to a small attic apartment hidden behind a secret door.

The door was opened. Inside, the fire brigade bore witness to sights and sounds that would forever haunt their souls. The odor, a mixture of suffering, sweat and decay, assaulted their senses—a stink so rich and thick it threatened to suffocate them. The room was dark, but from within the pitch, anguished cries, moans and groans punctuated the silence. The firemen, men who braved fire and death every day, hesitated to light their lanterns for fear of what the light might reveal. Experienced men, they were familiar with the scent of death and it was this aroma that stayed their hands now.

The cook pleaded with them to proceed and so they did. Their lanterns were lit, the glow revealing a carnival of the grotesque. The room was full of slaves, some dead, some not. Numerous corpses lay in varying states of decay, while the living survived in terrible and gruesome states of torture, testament to Lalaurie's brutal imagination. Victims were nude, tied down to fearsome-looking devices.

Those who were conscious considered the firefighters their saviors and begged for a quick death. The surviving victims were taken to hospital, but for most it was far too late. It's unclear how many died under Lalaurie's care. Slaves had been disappearing from her mansion for years but most people viewed this as evidence of Lalaurie's exacting standards. A search of the house revealed corpses hidden beneath the floorboards. All told, 12 deaths were attributed to the wicked madame.

News of Lalaurie's crimes spread, inciting anger and indignation in those who heard of her depravity. A mob formed and took to the streets, ready to mete out justice in the only way it could: through the hanging of Madame Delphine Macarty Lalaurie. With their torches blazing, the mob's calls for her head echoed through the French Quarter. The doors to the mansion were battered down and the horde looted and plundered its way through the building. Try as they might, though, the mob never found Lalaurie. A quick look in the carriage house revealed that it was empty. Lalaurie had fled New Orleans.

No one ever determined what happened to this most cruel of mistresses. There is speculation that she returned to her native France or sought refuge in the wilderness of Louisiana. Others believe that Lalaurie never fully abandoned New Orleans and returned to the city, undetected, under the name "Widow Blanque." She is said to have died in 1842, her body buried in New Orleans at an undisclosed location. In 1941, a grave marker plate for her tomb was found in St. Louis Cemetery. But the marker was not attached to a specific tomb, and her resting place remains as mysterious as the reasons for her madness. Regardless, her legacy lives on in her mansion and some believe that in death, she has returned to the house where such tragedy occurred.

With good reason, 1140 Royal Street stood abandoned for years after Lalaurie fled. Few wanted to be reminded of her particular brand of twisted evil. It seemed that within the house's walls, no one could forget the horror. The house was haunted and few wanted to live where lives were disrupted by the screams of agony descending from the now empty attic, by the apparitions of mutilated slaves who shuffled around, lost and scared, and by the suspicion that those who enter the house are never seen again. A man who later bought the property attempted to rent the rooms out to tenants but few ever honored their leases, choosing instead to abandon the house mere days after moving in. The business venture failed and it wasn't long before 1140 Royal Street stood empty once again.

But with space at a premium in New Orleans, the house was not vacant for long. Following the Civil War, it was reborn as an integrated high school until the former slave owners, who feared for their identities and culture, decided to expel the blacks and recast the school along segregationist lines. Inevitably, businesses didn't stay long at 1140 Royal Street. After the schools' failures, it was empty until the late 19th century when immigration to the state and city drove up demand for affordable housing. Enterprising landlords seized control of the house but soon found themselves struggling to keep their tenants, even though rooms throughout the city were scarce. Few wanted to live in a building where the supernatural exerts such a powerful force.

Tenants complained of being attacked by the ghost of a naked black man in chains, while pet owners would often return to their rooms to find their cats or dogs brutally butchered. Children learned to fear the house's halls, as they were patrolled by none other than Lalaurie herself, who kept at her ready at all times the whip with which she must have flogged so many to death. Lalaurie is seen throughout the mansion. Sadly, she appears to show no remorse for her actions. Without fail, she continues to flog the ghost of the slave girl who leapt to her death so many years ago. The slave girl's cries still echo throughout the building and its court-yard, standing as testament to Lalaurie's terrible cruelty. The house was left to rot once more.

Two more ventures failed at 1140 Royal Street—a saloon and a furniture store. The owner of the latter found it impossible to keep his furniture clean. He returned from a night's sleep to a store of items covered in a foul-smelling, viscous liquid. Again and again, the man's stock would be ruined. Fed up with the situation, he was determined to catch the vandals he believed responsible for the damage. Armed with a shotgun, he trained its barrels on the store's only accessible entrance and watched all evening. No one came, yet when the light of day filled the storeroom, the man was stunned to see that once again, everything had been sprayed with the foul liquid. The store closed that day.

After the house was divided into apartments, a retired physician bought it. Since that time, the house has been eerily quiet, as Lalaurie seems to have quit this mortal plane and found some sort of peace. But it's possible that peace will elude a spirit as wicked and as cruel as hers. Perhaps she is waiting, ever watchfully, for the proper time to return and trouble the living once more.

DeFeo House
AMITYVILLE, NEW YORK

Ronald "Butch" DeFeo turned the television off and stared into the darkness. He sat for just a few moments before getting up and walking up the stairs to his bedroom. He rummaged in his closet for a few seconds, feeling blindly behind piles of old sweaters and shirts until he found what he was looking for. The room lights were kept off so he wouldn't wake either of his parents or his two brothers and two sisters. He pulled a long narrow object from the closet, and it glinted ever so lightly in the light that managed to trickle in from the street. He left his room and began making his way around the house.

A short while later, Ronald walked into Henry's, a bar two blocks north of his house. He was hysterical and collapsed into the arms of concerned friends. His cries were nearly indiscernible at first, but certain words did stand out: blood, bodies, horror. Ronald led a group from Henry's back to his house. They walked through the front yard, past the sign that Ronald DeFeo Sr. had put up in the front yard to let Amityville know that his family had "High Hopes." When they got inside the house, the group saw what had driven Ronald so frantic.

Ronald's father, mother, two brothers and two sisters were all lying on their stomachs. Each one had been shot at close range with a .35 caliber rifle. They were all dead. The question, of course, was who committed this most horrible of crimes?

Police questioned the lone DeFeo survivor for information as to who might have killed his family. Ronald offered

Six in Family Found Slain
In Bedrooms in L.I. Home

AMITYVILLE, L. I., Nov. 13 —A well-to-do car dealer, his wife and four of his five children were found murdered in their beds tonight here on Long Island's South Shore... police

All six had been shot to death, according to James Caples, Chief of the Organized Crime Bureau of the Suffolk Police Department. He said however, that he was ... out death by shotg...

Brutal and apparently unplanned, the DeFeo murders made front-page headlines across America.

some theories. At 23, he had already developed a serious drug habit and had indulged in petty thievery—pursuits that landed him in the company of men with less than sterling reputations. Ronald claimed that he was a marked man, that the Mafia had sent a hit man to kill him. To the police, Ronald's story was questionable at best. There was little concrete evidence at the crime scene to prove the existence of the alleged hit man. What investigators found instead were signs that they should focus their efforts on just one man: Ronald DeFeo.

An empty gun box in Ronald's closet matched the murder weapon. Ronald was brought in for questioning again, and this time, under intense pressure, fissures began to appear in his story. As the interrogation wore on, the fissures widened, causing Ronald's account of the night in question to fall apart. Ronald then changed his stories a number of times, accusing his older sister of the act before finally confessing to the crime himself. But he refused to take full responsibility for his actions. He blamed the voices—the ones that only he could hear whenever he was in the house. They had ordered the killings, Ronald maintained. He was confident that the courts would find him insane when they heard his testimony. (Coincidentally, he was lucid enough to ask when he would be receiving the money from his family's life insurance.)

Ronald DeFeo was convicted and sentenced to six consecutive life sentences for his crimes. Yet it is his former home that has gained notoriety and fame as the years have passed. Few outside Amityville remember Ronald DeFeo's crimes. Many, though, can recall the controversy that Ronald created when he said that spirits possessed the DeFeo house at 112 Ocean Avenue.

Amityville was immortalized, for better or for worse, when the Lutz family moved into the DeFeo house. They arrived in 1975, a year after Ronald had shot his family to death. Twenty-eight days later, the Lutzes moved out and called a press conference. A curious public was treated to stories of how the Lutzes had been driven from their house, that demons and spirits were tormenting them. They described being roused from slumber every night, always at the time Ronald is believed to have killed his family.

During the day, ectoplasmic ooze and blood seeped from the walls. Flies swarmed the house, masses of them appearing in rooms as if by magic. A pig, bloodied and decaying, somehow made its way into the house, where it moved about not by walking, but by floating inexplicably from room to room.

The freakish apparition terrified the Lutz family and proved an eerily fitting accompaniment to the murderous feelings that haunted them—feelings that urged family members to reenact Ronald's crimes.

The house, moreover, appeared to have a will of its own. Doors and windows opened on their own, and there were times when rooms in the house would be bathed in a red glow. When they looked out the home's windows, the Lutzes found themselves staring into a pair of large glowing red eyes. Thoroughly spooked, the Lutzes left the home.

It wasn't long before Amityville became the destination of choice for ghost-hunters and paranormal investigators. They swarmed the town, all eager to catch a glimpse of the possessed home. Inevitably there were some who doubted the validity of the Lutzes' story.

In 1975, George Lutz was a bankrupt land surveyor. Many asked how he could afford to purchase the house at 112 Ocean Avenue, which, at $80,000, was well beyond his means. And it was. The Lutzes never made a single mortgage payment on the home, so in 1976 ownership reverted to Columbia Savings and Loans. After it became clear that the Lutzes were actively seeking bids for the rights to their story, skeptics began suspecting that the Lutzes had concocted the stories for profit. In short order, a soap opera writer named Jay Anson had written *The Amityville Horror: A True Story*. The book's success drew national attention to the case and spawned a Hollywood adaptation. The film, starring James Brolin and Margot Kidder, was released in 1979. As the story gained in popularity, so did the scrutiny of the Lutzes intensify.

Professional investigators had conducted thorough examinations of the home. Contrary to the Lutzes' claims, they believed that the home was not possessed, nor did it need to be exorcised. Of the experts, the most vocal was a Dr. Stephen Kaplan, who felt that there were simply too many discrepancies between the Lutzes' original accounts of life in Amityville and those described in Anson's book. He pointed out that during the entire time that the Lutzes were living in their demonic home, never once did they seek outside assistance from the police. Most damning of all, at least in Kaplan's eyes, was the fact that those who purchased the property after the Lutzes never reported anything unusual in the home at 112 Ocean Avenue.

Many believe now that the Amityville horror was nothing more than a hoax perpetrated by a couple looking for a quick fix to a money problem. Although people have lived in and out of the house without incident for many years, some investigators still believe that the house was possessed. Two of these are Ed and Lorraine Warren.

The Warrens investigated the home in 1978 and claim that the real hoax was the one offered by Kaplan. The Warrens believe that the Lutzes received very little money from the book and movie and that financial concerns did not motivate their coming forward with the story. The Warrens point to questions regarding Ronald's crime. He used a .35 caliber rifle, a weapon whose retort would have been loud enough to wake the DeFeos' neighbors. Incredibly, not even the DeFeo murder victims were woken up as Ronald went through the house shooting his family. The victims were in a state of phantomania, a paralysis that occurs when individuals are attacked by supernatural forces.

When Ed and Lorraine explored the home, both had experiences that they could only attribute to the existence of the paranormal. Ed was walking through the cellar when he saw shadows moving among thousands of blips of light. Suddenly the shadows were on top of him, trying to force him to the ground. When he resisted, he experienced a sensation as if something was trying to lift him off the ground.

For her part, Lorraine was almost paralyzed with fear even before she entered the home. When inside, Lorraine felt as if water was rushing all around her; the air in the home itself was thickening and becoming, in effect, a solid. As she moved from room to room, some still adorned with the DeFeos' furniture, Lorraine was overwhelmed by feelings of terror and fear. She described the sensation to the New England Society for Psychic Research as being "as close to Hell as [I'll] ever get."

If indeed the house was once haunted, then perhaps it is no longer. Of all those who have lived in the house since the Lutzes, no one has reported anything strange or unusual, but rather a growing disdain for the house's notoriety and the hordes of tourists drawn to it. The Warrens still maintain that the home was haunted, as do the Lutzes. Skeptics still charge that the stories were created to offer an explanation for Ronald's actions, that the Lutzes seized on the idea to rid themselves of bankruptcy. Regardless, the house at 112 Ocean Avenue captured the public imagination for years as the place where six people were brutally killed. Ronald DeFeo continues to serve six consecutive life sentences at Greenhaven Penitentiary in Stormville, New York.

Dagg Poltergeist
CLARENDON, QUEBEC

A poltergeist is literally a noisy spirit, yet such a simple definition fails to indicate that poltergeists, unlike most spirits, are cruel, malicious and destructive. They tend to prey upon the young and the precociously intelligent. No one knows why, but a poltergeist will latch on to one particular person, usually a young girl, and make her its agent and medium for communication. So it was with 11-year-old Dinah Maclean, a girl who had moved in with her adoptive family, the Daggs, to a farmhouse just off Gatineau Park Road in Clarendon, Quebec.

As she related to her parents later, Dinah had been sitting in the woodshed when she was pushed to the ground and held there by an unseen force; a disembodied voice then came out of the air. It sounded like an old man speaking. It was deep and guttural and promised that it would return to speak with her from time to time. Dinah was terrified and spent days in dread. Alone, she might hear a noise and then ask if anyone was there. There was never a reply.

The Daggs began to worry. Dinah was growing more agitated by the day and her appetite had dwindled to almost nothing. She moved about as if in a pall, growing thinner and paler until her family could bear it no longer. They pleaded with her, begging their daughter to confide in them and tell them what had happened. Dinah took her father, George Dagg, to the woodshed with her to show him what had happened.

Gingerly and almost imperceptibly, Dinah whispered, "Is anyone there?" The reply was swift and brutal. An irate voice claiming to be the Devil ordered the father out of the shed lest his neck be broken in an unfortunate accident. Not long after, the Dagg family found the security of their home and their lives in danger. It began innocently enough. Some of George's money disappeared, only to appear somewhere else. And then the situation became grotesque.

On the morning of September 15, 1889, the Daggs awoke and nearly gagged to death on the stench that had invaded their house. It was the smell of excrement; the floors of their farmhouse were covered in filth. It had been combined with sugar, rendering the mixture particularly thick and all the more difficult to remove. The doors were covered in the same revolting mess. But no sooner had the family managed to rid their home of the matter than they had to turn their attention to the kitchen.

Everything that wasn't bolted down or weighed down in the kitchen was throwing itself across the room. Pots, pans, pails and dishes all flew through the air as if propelled by invisible hands. Then they would suddenly drop to the ground as if they had hit a wall. The house rang with the terrible cacophony and the Daggs were at a loss over what to do. They put the pots, pans, pails and dishes away and then shut the cabinet doors. Once their backs were turned, however, the cabinets flung themselves open once more and the same items flew through the air again like a flock of geese taking flight. The Daggs cleaned the kitchen again, only to find that the rest of the house had fallen into disarray as well. Their chairs, sofa and kitchen table had all been turned upside down. The Daggs stared in disbelief and wonderment, asking themselves what they had done to deserve such a fate.

With their furniture back in place, the family murmured a prayer, hoping that they had seen the last of the demon. Alas, it was not to be. As they rested on the sofa, all the windows in their house shattered at once with a loud crash. Luckily for the Daggs, none of them had been sitting near a window; shards flew through the air like arrows, embedding themselves in the floor and walls. But if the Daggs considered this event the last of their problems, they were surely mistaken.

At least eight separate fires broke out through the house, testing the Daggs' resolve in their attempts to extinguish them. And as they rushed to fill buckets with water from their pump, the poltergeist assaulted them, pulling hair off their heads by the handfuls. Dinah's long brown braid barely clung to her head, held in place by the merest strands of hair. Patches of naked flesh dotted the scalps of the men, while their home was now decorated with a wall-to-wall carpeting of human hair.

As night fell, the house settled into an eerie calm. But the Daggs were unable to relax, still fearful that the poltergeist might return. Dinah was exhausted and she fell into her mother's lap. Within minutes, she was enjoying the rest that had been denied her for so long.

The other Daggs spent a restless night in their beds, waking up with a shock anytime they heard any noise. In the morning, they wondered if the events of the previous day had actually happened, but they knew that there was no denying them. Hair and glass still covered their floors, and parts of their home still bore burn marks from the eight fires that had burned through the afternoon.

Unsure of what to do, George Dagg rode to Plum Hollow, where a psychic and medium named Elizabeth Barnes lived.

He brought Barnes back to the house, hoping that she would be able to exorcise the demon from his house. Unfortunately, Barnes was unable to discern the exact cause of the possession and told the Daggs that they had been cursed. But when the Daggs asked by whom, Barnes couldn't say any more. Ironically enough, it was the demon that would provide the answers.

Seventeen witnesses signed affidavits that claimed that, through the young girl, the demon spoke with 20 people who had gathered to find out what was happening in the Dagg farmhouse. The demon claimed that the wife of a neighboring family, Mrs. Wallace, had sent him to curse the family. For what reason he did not know. Angered friends went and brought Mrs. Wallace to the farmhouse to confront her creation, but it soon became clear that the demon had not spoken the truth, and had only created the situation for his own amusement. A shaken Mrs. Wallace left the Dagg household that night. For the next five hours, the demon stayed with Dinah as the fascinated crowd drew in ever closer to hear the otherworldly voice. The demon soon grew tired of the game, but the crowd refused to yield. It was only when the demon began revealing intimate and private secrets about those in attendance that the crowd began to disperse.

George Dagg grew tired of this bizarre sideshow of the macabre. He feared for his daughter's life and wanted the demon exorcised as soon as possible. He summoned an Anglican priest to his farmhouse but the exorcism never took place. Before the priest could even begin, his Bible went missing. A thorough search of the house was conducted but the book was nowhere to be found. It had disappeared from the priest's hands, presumably for good. Shaking his head in puzzlement, the priest left the Dagg homestead, short one Bible. But when Mrs. Dagg made ready to fire the oven for that night's dinner, she drew back in surprise at what she saw lying inside the appliance. There, amidst the wood and ash, was the Bible. At that point, the Dagg house fairly shook as the demon roared that he would return the following Sunday.

The week was spent in tortured despair. While Dinah's spirits seemed to be lifting, one could only wonder how long it would last. The demon's return was all but assured and what then? What would become of the little girl? There was little they could do but wait.

Sunday arrived and the day was bright and warm. Throngs of people trampled about in the Daggs' fields, hoping to catch a glimpse of what had happened the week before. Word had spread through Clarendon about the Dagg demon and many had made the journey to the farm to see it for themselves. They would not be disappointed. The demon returned, speaking through the girl once again. It said that it would leave forever at midnight, but the crowd was so fascinated with its answers and its intelligence that they prevented the demon from leaving until well past the appointed time. It was three in the morning before the demon finally gave Dinah back to her worried family.

The next morning, as the three Dagg children rose and went outside to play, they saw, high above them, bright against the deep blue of the cloudless sky, a white angel ascending to heaven. Only the children saw the being. But George and his wife knew as they watched their adopted daughter Dinah recover her strength, her color and the smile that could brighten the darkest of days that the poltergeist had abandoned them forever.

2
Waking the Dead

When people move into a house or renovate, they look forward to something new. In some homes, however, moving and renovating are cues for the paranormal. Previously free of paranormal disturbances, a number of houses become venues for spirits awakened from eternal rest by disturbances in what were once their homes. Sometimes the changes are welcome, while at other times they simply serve to agitate the restless spirit— just something for you to consider if your kitchen needs new fixtures or if the children are clamoring for a pool.

General Lee's Home
ALEXANDRIA, VIRGINIA

General Robert E. Lee is best remembered as the Civil War general who led the Confederates to victory at the 2nd Bull Run and Fredericksburg, who masterfully brought Union troops to a standstill at Antietam, but who was turned back infamously at Gettysburg. His surrender to the armies of Grant at Appomattox, Virginia, signaled the end of the Civil War. Though plagued by heart disease, Lee spent the last years of his life pleading for peace amidst the tumult of Reconstruction. On October 12, 1870, the former general died; North and South both mourned his passing.

Those who wish to see the general today travel to Lexington, Virginia, where his body is buried. But for those interested in a more memorable or tangible experience, a trip to his boyhood home in Alexandria is in order. No one has any definitive proof that it is indeed his spirit that haunts the house at 607 Oronoco Street, but there are theories proposing that the ghost might be that of his son or brother, both of whom died when they were four. Of course, if the ghost of 607 Oronoco is a child, how could it be the resurrected spirit of Robert Lee? Perhaps the general chose to return to a time of innocence, to days untainted by the blood of brothers. Who among us hasn't looked back on childhood with nostalgia for simpler times? The ghost who inhabits Lee's former home is happy, laughing as he plays childish pranks on the living. If it is Lee, the old general is relishing his rediscovered innocence.

In 1962, Henry Koch bought the historic house that had not only served as Lee's home for nine years, but had also

The identity of the spirit in General Robert E. Lee's former Virginia home remains unclear.

received George Washington on a number of occasions. The Koch family's experiences with the house's permanent resident were related to psychic-sensitive Suzy Smith. Upon visiting the Lee home, Smith reported that as she approached the end of the downstairs hallway, she felt a "prickly sensation along [her] spine. It wasn't scary…it was more like the delicious chill you get when someone kisses your ear or the back of your neck." She made sure to tell the Kochs about her feelings; they, in turn, told her that many others who knew nothing about the house had experienced the same thing in exactly the same spot.

The Kochs first encountered the spry spirit on moving day. Walking through the main hallway, husband and wife heard laughter and footsteps from upstairs. They figured that their seven-year-old son, William, was getting acquainted with his new surroundings. They were shocked when William came running, not down the stairs as they had expected, but from behind them from somewhere on the first floor. In truth, he had been nowhere near the upstairs floor.

The Kochs found that their days in the house were often accompanied by what they could only describe as the sound of a giggling child running up and down the stairs. At night, the house would fall under an eerie silence, as if the ghost were being held to a rigid curfew. In the light of day, the family would hear the child two or three times a day and noted that the spirit liked to walk with them, laughing along the way. If the family was sitting down to dinner, the doorbell would ring. Of course, when the door was opened, nobody would be there. Objects acquired the ability to disappear on their own, only to turn up somewhere else completely unexpected days later.

Mrs. Koch once described how a cigarette lighter of hers went missing. Try as she might, she could not find it anywhere—that is, until the day she was walking down the hall and she saw the missing lighter flung in her direction from unseen hands. It landed at her feet with a clatter. Mrs. Koch could only stare at it, wavering between awe and surprise.

The Kochs longed to find out more about what was taking place in their home, but wanted to avoid any sort of public ridicule. It wasn't until they had a conversation with their milkman that the mystery began to unravel. The milkman approached the family and casually asked if they had heard from the little Lees. With their collective sanity no longer in question, the Kochs happily answered the question. They were not alone in believing that the house was haunted. But that recognition didn't make it any easier for them to discuss the paranormal happenings with close friends unfamiliar with the house's history.

Mr. Koch was entertaining guests one evening when their conversation was interrupted by a guitar. Someone upstairs was playing the instrument beautifully. Mr. Koch knew that there had to be something amiss. He was supportive in most everything his children did, but he knew that his daughter couldn't play so well. She was still having trouble picking the chords for "Hot Cross Buns." What the group was hearing were the strummings of someone with far more ability than Koch's daughter. His friends wondered who could play so well and asked their host. Not wanting to frighten his guests by saying it was the ghost, he told them it was his daughter. Later that evening, Koch's suspicions were confirmed. His daughter hadn't even brought her guitar home. It was stowed away in her locker at school.

Guests were at the house again to witness what was perhaps the strangest event ever to take place there. It was a Sunday afternoon and everyone had congregated in the sitting room. A woman was speaking when she noticed, along with everyone else, snow falling. The snow itself wasn't unusual, except that it was falling inside the house from

To this day, a giggling child is heard running up and down the stairs in General Lee's former home.

just two feet overhead. Within minutes, the woman was soaking wet and cold. The men checked to see if perhaps the snow had been blowing in from outside or from the ceiling, but a thorough examination revealed that all windows and doors were closed and that there were no holes in the ceiling. As hard as it was to believe, the snowfall was entirely localized in the house, above the head of one unfortunate guest. She took it all in stride but was ready to leave a short while later. Just as she was about to set foot outside the front door, the snow fell once again.

Could all the strange events taking place in Lee's boyhood home be attributed to his spirit? If not, there are others in the house keeping him company. Many have reported seeing a black dog with a wagging tail running through the yard. As soon as the animal is approached, it disappears. More recently, people have claimed that two young girls, quite possibly his little sisters, both of whom died very young, have joined the Lee ghost.

People are still unsure about the identity of the youthful spirit haunting 607 Oronoco. Lee had a child who died at age four, but that death took place 50 miles away, so it's unlikely that the child would return to a home he never knew. Regardless, it is generally believed that a Lee haunts the house, which would clarify why the spirit is often referred to as "the Lees." Whether the lone spirit is the reincarnation of Robert or Philip seems to be a matter of taste.

Lyons Tavern
NORTH WOODSTOCK, CONNECTICUT

Long ago, in this land of pastoral tranquility, there stood a grand farmhouse. Although the setting was rural, the farmhouse's flavor was distinctly more cosmopolitan. With 16 rooms, the farmhouse was well equipped to operate as an inn. It drew visitors from throughout the Northeast eager for a drink and a place to stay. Named after its builder, Lyons Tavern was a popular place for years. The Revolutionary War, however, took its toll, and while a nation fought to survive its infancy, trips to the country were no longer a priority. But even more devastating than the conflict was an unforeseen family tragedy.

One of the Lyon children, a 14-year-old daughter, fell ill. With almost all family and friends tied up in the Revolutionary War effort, the sick child was, more often than not, left on her own in the vast emptiness of the farmhouse. Her mother would sometimes return from her work in the fields to check on her and bring her anything she might need.

One day, she prepared to bring her daughter some water and a bit of soup, arranging a cup, bowl and spoon on a wooden tray. A single daisy completed the setting and she walked to her daughter's room. The door was closed, which the mother found odd. When she had last checked on her, not less than an hour earlier, she had left the door open; it was then easier for her to hear if the girl needed anything. The mother set the tray on the floor and eased the door open to reveal an empty room. Where had her daughter gone? Mrs. Lyons began walking around the farmhouse, looking through all its rooms and closets but finding nothing. Her sick daughter had disappeared. The girl was never seen again.

Little is known of the tavern's history after the Lyons moved away. A succession of owners came and went, but their particular histories were lost. In 1951, the Viner family came to North Woodstock and liked the look of the farmhouse. Despite its rotting timbers and sagging walls, they decided that the home's restoration would become their mission. After weeks of work, the Viners moved into the fully restored and renewed farmhouse. They didn't stay long. Their renovations had awakened the spirits of the past, and when events beyond explanation began happening throughout the house, Mrs. Viner was inspired to investigate.

What the Viners heard in their house was this: the pounding of hurried footsteps up the staircase, the muffled sounds of a struggle from a second-floor bedroom, then two very loud thumps. What Mrs. Viner found was this: cold spots in bedrooms and underneath wallpaper she had removed to paint the walls, blood stains. Mrs. Viner had the pieces to a puzzle but had no clue how to put them together. Plunging into the past, she learned that the farmhouse was once a tavern, and, naturally, the site of many a drunken brawl.

Mrs. Viner discovered that two regulars to the Lyons Tavern had long ago decided that the best part about the establishment wasn't the atmosphere, the accommodations, the food or even the drink. The best part was the pretty barmaid with whom they both had fallen in love—or at least lust. Every night, they would pull out their favorite seats from the bar, sit down and begin vying for the affection and attention of the waitress who sent their pulses racing.

One particular night, the men had had a little too much to drink. As the night progressed, their enmity festered, fueled by alcohol and fanned by passion. It wasn't long before the two were trading insults and then blows. They were ordered to leave the tavern, but instead of heading home they retired to an upstairs room where they continued their squabble. Swords were drawn and before long both men were dead, their blood spattered on the walls of the room like paint. The Viners' restoration had restored life to the dead. What the family heard as they sat in their home was a faithful recreation of a quarrel that had gone horribly wrong almost 250 years before.

The disruptions became more frequent and intrusive. Soon enough, it became impossible to maintain any semblance of normalcy. The footsteps grew louder and more insistent. The recurring replay of the fatal struggle was too much to bear for the Viners. In 1961, they abandoned the home that they had so lovingly restored.

Waverley Mansion
COLUMBUS, MISSISSIPPI

To look upon Waverley Mansion is to see the history of Columbus, Mississippi, writ small. It is the grandest of mansions, a study in opulence rendered in four stories and white painted pine. To walk its grand staircase, ascending 65 feet from its bottom step to the crown of the mansion's dome, is to walk back in time. Remarkably, just 50 years previous the elegant home was decrepit. Vegetation had invaded and vagrants had moved in. The house's floors were buried beneath years of leaves, branches, garbage and other waste. Vagrants slept where once the elite of Columbus social circles had walked in their finest dress. Everything changed when Robert and Donna Snow decided to resuscitate Waverley and restore the mansion to its former glory. But during its renovations, strange things began happening—occurrences the couple could only attribute, in the end, to the presence of spirits from Waverley's storied past.

Columbus became prosperous as most cities in the South had: through the production of cotton and various other crops grown on vast plantations worked by slaves. Settlers had been drawn to the fertile area by its black soil; it was ideal for growing cotton, which was then shipped to eastern states depleted of the crop. In the years leading up to the Civil War, Columbus thrived.

One of those attracted to its promise of wealth in return for a little hard labor was George Hampton Young, a colonel from Georgia. In 1852, he began construction of a home along a gentle knoll that sat near the Tombigbee River. Six years later, with the assistance of architect Charles Pond and artisan Richard Miller, the mansion was completed. Its crowning touches were English boxwoods that Mrs. Young, who died before the home's completion, had planted at the entrance. The plants are there still today, now more than 150 years old. The home was large, but Young had a family of ten that needed all the space.

Just three years later, Young's plantation resembled a small village. With over 1000 laborers, it was easy to understand why he needed to construct a post office, a brick kiln, a cotton gin, an ice house, a lumber mill and a leather tannery. As for his family, he built massive gardens for them, as well as marble-lined swimming pools that dotted the 40 acres of his plantation. Waverley became the social center of Columbus, with weekly dances held in its grand ballroom. But everything changed when batteries operating under the orders of the newly formed Confederate States of America opened fire upon Fort Sumter in North Carolina.

Although Federal troops never occupied Columbus, it was the state's capital while Jackson burned to the ground; the city was devastated by the transition from an economy with slaves to one without. Waverley was no different. Young died in the home in 1888 and successive generations of Young children kept Waverley occupied until Captain William Young, the youngest child, died there in 1913. Waverley then sat abandoned for years, its 40 acres slowly being reclaimed from agriculture by encroaching overgrowth, until the Snow family of Philadelphia arrived and began their work. The home today is listed as a National Historic Landmark.

The question remains: was the home ever completely abandoned? Ghosts had been seen in and around the house

Ghosts have been spotted in and around Waverley Mansion in Mississippi for many years.

since the last Young passed away. There is also the mythical figure of Major John Pytchlyn, who died in 1835 after living an orphaned life under the care of the Choctaw Indians. It's said that he loved riding his horse near the Tombigbee River, and on his sojourns often passed through the property that became the Young plantation. Perhaps he still rides horse near the Tombigbee River to this day.

According to witnesses, it begins with the faint sound of pounding hooves in the distance. They grow louder and louder until the earth shudders underfoot. And then there he goes—brushing by but causing no stir in the air. The hoof-beats fade, leaving witnesses to wonder if the passing phantom was just the figment of an overactive imagination. The reaction is similar for those who see strangers when gazing into Waverley's mirrors. Colonel George Hampton Young, still a man of impeccable Southern charm, has been known to appear in mirrors throughout the house.

It is little surprise, then, that the Snows began hearing a mysterious little girl calling out for her mother. Mrs. Snow first heard the voice two years after she had moved into the mansion. She was sitting in an armchair when she heard a plaintive voice crying "Mama! Mama!" from somewhere outside. Mrs. Snow put her book down and walked to the open balcony door. She peered out over its edge, ready to greet one of her own children but saw nothing but the manicured lawn. When she asked her children about it later over supper, not a single one could recall having been outside or calling for their mother. Mrs. Snow might have thought one of her children was playing a prank on her, but over the years she continued to hear the voice every day in the afternoon. Although the plaintive voice no longer startled her, it did begin to concern her. She wondered what could have upset the phantom child so much. It was a mystery that would never be solved.

After five years, the ghost became more assertive. She began following Mrs. Snow about the house, calling out to her from different parts of the home. Far from unwelcome, the pitter-patter of the ghostly feet became a soothing accompaniment to Mrs. Snow's days. And then, every once in a while at night, Mrs. Snow would be roused from slumber by her children. They would ask her if the ghostly little girl was all right because they could hear her crying throughout the house. Mrs. Snow hoped that the little girl was safe and comfortable. She was relieved to spot the indentation of a small figure seemingly asleep in one of the mansion's four-poster beds.

Then, as Mrs. Snow was preparing dinner one day, she felt someone brush up against her. She turned but no one was there, and from out of the silence, came the voice. "Mama! Mama!" the girl cried, more desperate and distressful than ever before. Mrs. Snow was concerned, but all she could do was ask the girl what was wrong. That was the last the Snows heard from the girl for years. While she was absent from their lives, the Snows attempted to discover who the little girl might be but never came close to unraveling the mystery.

Ten years later, there was a break. Mrs. Snow was walking by the four-poster bed so favored by the little girl when she noticed that something was lying on it. She had made the bed carefully that morning and now there was an indentation in it. The little girl was back.

Even now, the little girl still makes an occasional appearance at Waverley. Many have caught a glimpse of her little spirit walking the halls in her nightgown, tresses of dark blond hair cascading over her shoulders. Her identity remains a mystery, but she is as much a part of Waverley as George Hampton Young, an important name in Columbus' fascinating past.

Firkins House
EDMONTON, ALBERTA

Spanning 158 acres, Fort Edmonton Park is Canada's largest historical park, faithfully recreating distinct eras in Edmonton's history with a mixture of original and replicated buildings and costumed interpreters. Seventy historical buildings dot the parkland, some dedicated to Edmonton in the late 19th century, others to the city as it was in 1905 and 1920. Visitors marvel at the close attention to detail and thrill at the idea of a journey back in time. It's said that the past comes alive in the park, but who knew that it could do so literally?

In 1985, Rod and Audrey Karpetz moved into a house on Saskatchewan Drive. Built in 1912, the home had only five previous owners, and, interestingly, none ever made a single change to it. So when the Karpetzes bought the building, they were buying an almost perfectly preserved example of early 20th-century architecture, its original Edwardian fixtures still intact. Seven years later, the novelty of owning the home had faded. It was a great challenge to live in a home where modern amenities such as plumbing, heating, insulation and electricity all depended upon fixtures and equipment installed 80 years ago. The inconvenience prompted the Karpetzes to make an important decision. Their home was unique; but how could they build themselves a new home without compromising the character and integrity of their old one? Their solution was simple. It would be donated to Fort Edmonton Park, where the home would be forever preserved.

And so in 1992 the historical park added a new (and old) building to its attractions. The home was christened the Firkins House, in honor of its first owners. It was carefully transported from Saskatchewan Drive to the park. Unfortunately, the move further stressed an already dilapidated home. Repairs were desperately needed, so the Fort Edmonton Historical Foundation mounted a fundraising effort to secure the money necessary for a complete restoration. A chance meeting between the foundation's executive director and a representative of the Edmonton military base allowed the work to move forward. Soldiers from the First Combat Engineer Regiment repaired and resurrected a home affected by years of neglect. As the soldiers labored, they realized that the historical foundation had bought more than just a house. Something had moved along with the building to Fort Edmonton Park. The Firkins House was haunted.

Before the move, the Firkins House's resident spirit was said to be quite content and compassionate. One former resident of the home claimed that the ghost sang lullabies to her baby. The baby responded with smiles and coos before drifting off to sleep. Other residents reported seeing the ghost of a young man sitting at the kitchen table and added that sometimes the ghost would jump upon them. It would stop singing whenever the mother checked on the room, only to start again once she left. No one really knows who the ghost is, although there were rumors once that he was a young man who died while living at the house. What is certain is that during and after the move, the ghost became more mischievous and workers were hard-pressed to explain what was going on all around them.

Before the house was transported to the park, all its windows were shut securely. Workers who entered the home upon its arrival at the park found all its windows wide open. The befuddlement continued when tools began disappearing. Workers discovered that their hammers and chisels were never quite where they left them, and finding them became a daily chore. While searching for their equipment, they often heard strange and unexplained noises issuing forth from different rooms in the house. When the rooms were searched, nothing was amiss, save for the inescapable and unmistakable scent of lilacs that hung heavily in the air. All the workers felt slightly uncomfortable in the building; they always felt as if someone, or something, was watching them. Someone was.

A radiator fell over, as if pushed by invisible hands. An upstairs room was empty, and somehow a window that had already been nailed into the wall fell to the ground six meters below. Surprisingly, not one of the four panes broke. It was as if someone had pulled the window out from its frame and placed it gently upon the ground. At other times, doors that swung open easily one moment wedged themselves tightly into the doorjambs moments later. Although its identity remains a mystery, the Firkins House ghost was alive and well, and quite obviously interested by all the activity taking place within his home. A visit to Fort Edmonton Park might very well exceed anyone's wildest expectations should the Firkins House ghost decide to make an appearance. His presence gives new meaning to the term "living history."

Gehm House
ST. LOUIS, MISSOURI

Greed is a powerful force. It can compel some individuals to kill. It can inspire others to pursue the American Dream. At times, it is even powerful enough to resurrect the dead. And so it is inside Gehm House where eccentric owner Henry Gehm, who died over 50 years ago, still walks about the house, forever seeking what is, according to legend, his hidden pockets of gold coins.

Bart Adams had built Gehm House on Plant Avenue in St. Louis to serve as his summer retreat. Gehm, a German immigrant, moved into the home in 1906, and from the start he was a figure of some mystery. Gehm was a loner, a man who preferred his own company to anyone else's. Neighbors who rarely saw him branded him an eccentric. Little is known for certain about the man, but he is believed to have worked on the railroad, leasing cars to the various traveling circuses that crisscrossed the country by rail. Gehm died in 1944, from terminal cancer of the spine; he would reveal more about himself in death than he had in life.

In 1956, the Furry family moved into Gehm House. The couple, with two young daughters in tow, could not have possibly anticipated what would happen next. They hadn't lived in the house long before they were treated to a constant cacophony of pounding footsteps on their second floor and thumps at their windows. Had they been able to find a concrete cause for the noise, they might have been able to solve the problem, but whenever they heard the footsteps, all family members were accounted for and the only explanation was that someone or something was walking through the house. Whenever there was a thump on the window, the Furrys would look out, only to see nothing but their yard. But while these problems plagued the entire family, Mrs. Furry was subjected to her own special brand of harassment.

Every night at two in the morning, she would be shaken by unseen hands rattling her headboard, sometimes so violently that she would wake up convinced that the headboard had been broken in two. But whenever she awoke and she peered into the darkness, she saw nothing. The headboard bore not even a mark. The room was empty. A move from the house was discussed, but the Furrys had invested far too much of their time and money to abandon the home just yet. So they remained in the house for nine years. They moved in 1961, spurred by the need for a larger home and by the disturbing revelation from the Furry children that a ghostly woman in black had taken to beating them with a broom. While the children claimed that the paddlings never hurt, the Furrys weren't about to share space with a ghost who saw fit to abuse their children. Mr. Furry rushed into his daughter's bedroom one evening out of fear when he saw a glowing white shape enter the room. But when he opened the door and went in, he saw nothing unusual. Two questions continued to linger with them long after they left Gehm House. Who was the lady in black? And why was she spanking the children with her broom?

These questions also occurred to the next family that moved into Gehm House, the Walshes. As with the Furrys, their first few days in the home passed without interruption. But then, one evening, Clare Walsh was preparing dinner in the kitchen when she noticed that the family dog was acting just a little strangely. The animal was whimpering and cowering, obviously terrified of something. She turned around to see what it was. In the kitchen doorway was a ghost, a shimmering white haze with the shape and form of a human being. Only human beings don't just disappear into the thin air as this apparition did, moments after it floated into the room.

Mrs. Walsh did her best to forget what had happened. A period of calm followed this first sighting, and it was easy to believe that it was just an isolated incident. But then came the footsteps. And the thumps at the windows. Mrs. Walsh was determined to find out exactly what was going on inside her home and sought the counsel of her neighbors. Over dinner one evening, she learned that her neighbors were ready years ago to buy Gehm House but decided not to on the basis of advice from those in the area who knew both Gehm and his home's haunted reputation. Her neighbors directed Mrs. Walsh to a man who had lived in the neighborhood for years who would be able to supply the Walshes with more information. When Mrs. Walsh spoke with the man, she learned that Henry Gehm preferred to be alone for a reason.

The Great Depression wrought great misery on many across America; Gehm was one of them. After the economy had recovered and Gehm had pulled himself back from the brink of bankruptcy, he began to amass a new, albeit smaller, fortune in the railcar business. But Gehm had lost his trust in financial institutions and refused to leave his money with any of them. What he did instead was convert his holdings into gold coins that he took to squirreling away in different places throughout his house. Lest their locations be discovered, he kept them to himself. He was so protective of his coins that Gehm returned after death to watch over his investments.

Mr. Walsh had come down with the flu. To keep herself from becoming sick, Mrs. Walsh slept in the spare bedroom near the attic. That night, she tossed and turned as she was repeatedly awakened by the opening and closing of the attic door and the sounds of footsteps going in and out of the room. Mrs. Walsh quickly concluded that it must be the ghost walking in and out of the room. To make sure, she awoke one morning, closed the attic door and then went downstairs to work in the kitchen. When she returned to the attic hours later, the door was closed but everything in the room had been moved about. A chest sat with its drawers open, their contents scattered about the floor. Mrs. Walsh couldn't help but notice that these were blueprints across the attic floor and that they bore the name Henry Gehm.

The mess wasn't limited to the attic. The Walshes' bedroom was in a constant state of disarray as Gehm's ghost went through dressers and closets, leaving clothing scattered in his wake. Not surprisingly, this bedroom was where Gehm once slept. As the hauntings increased in intensity (lights turned on and off by themselves, screams came out of the darkness), the Walshes decided that they would leave the house. Gehm had driven away another family.

Another family eventually bought the home, and it continues to serve as a private residence. But if rumors are to be believed, it is as haunted as ever. Gehm remains convinced that his gold must be guarded at all costs. As for the woman in black, she is just one of a number of spirits who still haunt Gehm House and whose origins remain a mystery still. It's reasonable to assume that the other ghosts get along with Gehm. Otherwise, he very well might have driven them out long, long ago.

Locust Point
LOCUST POINT, MARYLAND

Locust Point is a neighborhood closely tied to its past. Homes stay within families for generations as they are passed down from parents to children. Families are close, united by a common past in which immigrants from Germany, Poland and Ireland came to the community to work the factories and the ports. Little has changed since Locust Point's inception in the 19th century; it is still a blue-collar town that displays its working-class roots proudly.

Stories are precious here too. Like heirlooms, they too have been passed down along with the historic homes. One in particular has entertained the residents of Locust Point for centuries now. It concerns the haunting of a pre-Civil War house that is still inhabited by one of its very first tenants.

Among the scores of immigrants who came to Locust Point was an English family. The decision to leave England was the husband's, a man who, unlike his wife, had not been born into a family with social standing. His was a commoner's background, and as a youth growing up in London— a city stratified by class and birth—the American promises of liberty and equality, of self-creation and the elimination of class, were impossible to resist. Shunned by his in-laws, who resented their daughter marrying beneath her class, the husband whisked his family away to the shores of the United States, eager to claim his fortune. He would return to British shores a self-made man, a man wealthy both in heart and in wallet, as well as a worthy husband.

The family arrived in America after a journey across the Atlantic in the cramped confines of a steamer. Days inside the cramped hold were not improved by the chilly air of the Atlantic. The husband did all he could to bolster his family's lagging confidence in his choice to leave the comfort and security of their home in Great Britain. Unfortunately, some passengers had carried unforgiving illnesses into the poorly ventilated chambers of the ship. The husband fell ill, forcing his desperate wife and her two children to nurse him back to health. But he was beyond their ability to heal, and before they even reached the shores about which he had dreamed for so long, he was dead, his body deposited beneath the waves of the Atlantic.

The rest of the family made their way to Locust Point. With what little money she had left, the wife rented a home in the area for her and her children. Within months, the money was gone. There was nothing left for food, for clothing, for even the most basic essentials. And so the family began to die slowly.

Pride can be a horrible thing. It can paralyze and blind individuals, leaving them unable and unwilling to do that which is necessary to secure their well-being, both spiritual and physical. And so it was with the wife and her small children. Pride prevented the woman from asking those in her neighborhood for help. Pride kept her from asking her disapproving family in London for support. Pride compelled her to stay in Locust Point, instead of returning home where she could have been taken care of and looked after. So she stayed in her house, keeping her children close to her as she rocked slowly in her rocking chair, trying harder and harder to keep herself and her children warm.

Neighbors became concerned when they realized that they hadn't seen the woman for days. Unsure of what to do, they finally decided that going into the house was the only option. They broke down the door and found inside the woman asleep in her rocking chair, with her children cradled in her arms. Of course, the family was sleeping the sleep of ages. They were buried in a paupers' graveyard. Their passing caused barely a ripple in the community; the wife had been shy and insular. But when a new family moved into the recently vacated home, the wife would return in a way no one could have ever imagined.

In 1865, the Boidie family became the new tenants. They immediately realized that something wasn't quite right inside the house. The first evening there, Mr. Boidie was walking up the stairs with a lantern. As he walked onto the third step, he suddenly felt cold and found himself standing in darkness. The lantern had been snuffed out. He felt his way back down the stairs to relight the wick. Upon doing so, he began up the stairs once again, felt the same isolated cold spot on the third step, but this time made sure to protect his lantern from any stray gust of wind that might have blown it out. His efforts were to no avail. Surely as the sun will rise, the lantern went out again. And again. And again. No matter what he did, he couldn't carry any light past the third step without its flame being extinguished.

Sleep escaped the Boidies that night as well. The family was serenaded at all hours by a cacophony of screams and wails that sent the children, terrified, to their parents' beds. Returning home from dinner at a friend's, the family was stunned to see the silhouette of a woman in a rocking chair in their front window. They rushed to the front room, which

The pier at Locus Point, Maryland, was a common landing point for many immigrants.

was empty save for a dining room table and chairs. There was no sign of a woman or a rocking chair. That night, the Boidies decided that they were going to leave their haunted house. If they were not welcome, they would not stay.

But the family's plans to leave had to be delayed when one of the Boidie children fell ill with typhoid fever. The doctor warned against the stress of moving and the havoc it might play with his recovery. The child was quarantined in a main-floor bedroom, confined to bedrest until he got better. The family was eager to move, but wasn't about to jeopardize the life of one of their own to do so.

One evening, the Boidies had just sat down to dinner when a scream and what sounded like a slap interrupted their meals. The sounds came from the bedroom of their sickly son. Mrs. Boidie raced to the bedroom to see what was happening. Her son told her that a woman had appeared before him and slapped him in the face. Not long after, other family members began experiencing slaps at all hours of both day and night. The Boidies could not uncover why the spirit of the home chose to treat them so harshly. In addition to the physical abuse, the nights were filled with unearthly howls and screams, inhuman by nature. It's a testament to the strength and resolve of the human spirit that the Boidie child was able to survive both illness and paranormal torment. The Boidies moved out of the home just days after their son recovered from typhoid.

The home that the Boidies vacated is still inhabited. It bears little resemblance to the house in which a mother's pride destroyed her family and tormented another. No one knows why, but activity in the house became decidedly less confrontational with the passage of time. As the years have rolled by, perhaps the proud mother has learned humility and now passes her time sobbing, not slapping.

Garfield House
HIRAM, OHIO

Bruno Mallone sat in his favorite armchair, worn but still serviceable, watching America's favorite sport, baseball. The seventh inning stretch had just begun, so Mallone reached down to the table next to his chair for his glass of soda. As he wrapped his hand around it the strangest thing happened. The glass jumped from his grasp. Mallone leaned over and stared down at the glass that was now resting quietly. He shrugged, convincing himself that he must have imagined the incident. He reached for it again, but this time there was no denying what happened. Mallone watched in amazement as the glass, like some sort of lemming, hopped across the table and then jumped off the edge where its contents spilt across the floor. Mallone was flabbergasted.

His family had been telling him for months that the house was haunted, but he had remained skeptical. He had questioned their stories about lights turning themselves on and off, random cold spots in otherwise well-insulated and well-heated rooms and objects that moved under their own power. As he watched the liquid from his upended glass spread across his floor, Mallone could no longer call himself a skeptic. He had witnessed the paranormal with his very own eyes.

The house in which the Mallone family lived had a long and distinguished history. Built in the Greek Revival style, the mansion was first constructed in 1836 to be used as a boarding house for faculty members of the Western Reserve Eclectic Institute. It was used as such until 1867 when the institute closed down. A succession of owners came and went until 1907, when Marcia Henry, a professor of English, Latin and Greek at Hiram College, bought the house.

Henry wanted to ensure that the building remain in her family after her death, so she willed it to her nephew Charles Henry, promising that she would return to the house after she died. Henry had no use for the home and instead donated it to the college to which his aunt had given so many years of her life. But when the college sold the home to the Mallones in 1961, they set in motion events that few could have anticipated. The Mallones did not just buy a house; they bought a living, breathing entity.

The Mallones loved the house but didn't like its location on the campus of Hiram College. They moved the home to its present location on a hill overlooking Garfield Road at the edge of town. The Mallones couldn't have known it, but the move and subsequent restoration of the house woke the spirits of those who had long ago passed into the world of shadow.

As soon as they moved in, the Mallones discovered the laws of nature and physics ceased to apply inside the house. When they went out for the night, the Mallones would go through the three-story structure to make sure that all the lights were off. Satisfied that everything was in order, the family would leave for the night. Much to their great surprise they would return to an illuminated home. As careful as they were to turn out the lights, one in particular refused to stay off. The dining room light was always on when they came home for some inexplicable reason. And, for a while, it was the same with their bedroom lights. The Mallones spent many nights staring at lamps and overhead lights that flickered to life without fail each and every night at 3:20, as if on a timer. Mr. Mallone was convinced that the problems had to do with faulty wiring, but electricians never found a cause. The wiring wasn't his only concern.

Some mornings, sleepy members of the family would pad into the washrooms and stare dumbly as they watched faucets turn themselves on. New taps were bought and installed, yet still they ran, an overture to days full of eerie events. Evenings were spent watching objects make their way across rooms, marveling at how a candle could fall off a mantle, land in the middle of the room with pinpoint accuracy and then hoist itself up onto a love seat.

Strange aromas with no visible source floated through the house. Mrs. Mallone often found herself struggling with watery eyes and fits of coughing as she tried to escape clouds of cigar smoke. Of course, the real question was, where did the cigar smoke come from? After all, no one in her family smoked them and if they did, it would be a simple matter of asking the offender to put it out. But she smelled cigars even when alone in the mansion and could only wonder who was still smoking from beyond the grave.

Mr. Mallone didn't smoke cigars. He didn't like them, but he did like doing the crossword puzzle that came every day with his newspaper. He could lose himself in the clues and he always felt some degree of personal satisfaction whenever he completed one, regardless of how many reference books he had been forced to consult. So it began to be a great annoyance when he discovered that somehow, someone was completing the puzzles before him. The mystery only deepened when he realized that the handwriting before him was unfamiliar, matching neither his wife's nor his daughter's. But Pam, his daughter, had problems of her own.

Even in the afterlife, Lucretia Garfield laments her unhappy marriage to James Garfield.

Any photographs or posters that she put up on her walls never hung for long. She lost track of how many times she came into her room to find all photographs and posters piled neatly in stacks on the floor. She would put them up only to have to repeat the process all over again. Then, one night, her room became so cold that she woke up, shivering and chattering. She had just set a foot on the floor to go get another set of blankets when a figure she took for her mother appeared, blankets in hand, and proceeded to tuck Pam into her bed. Pam thanked her mother and drifted back into sleep. The next morning, Pam again offered her thanks to her mother over breakfast. But Mrs. Mallone told her daughter that it couldn't have been her who tucked her in. She spent the night fast asleep and couldn't recall having been in Pam's room. The family was used to this sort of thing by now, so Pam just chewed her toast thoughtfully.

To be sure, the woman from her room looked nothing like her mother. But who was it? Driven by curiosity and a hunch, Pam thumbed through an old faculty yearbook that had been left in the house when they moved in. Faces flew by in a blur of black and white when Pam spotted one among the multitudes that was all too familiar. Holding the book closely, Pam read out the name beneath the face. "Marcia Henry," she whispered. "It was Marcia Henry."

With the spirit identified, the Mallones were intrigued and wanted to know more. They consulted with psychics Lorraine and Ed Warren who paid a visit to the home. The psychics concluded that there were indeed spirits in the house but that Marcia Henry was definitely not alone.

They sensed the presence of at least two other spirits. One was a thin, small woman who wheezed and coughed as if plagued with respiratory problems. She wore a long flowing gown that could not hide the sadness and isolation that resulted from an estrangement from her husband. In the master bedroom, there was another woman—a pretty individual with a confident aura. At the Warrens' suggestion, the Mallones left a tape recorder running in an empty room and returned a half-hour later. They played the tape back, expecting to hear nothing but static, but were stunned when they heard a man and woman speaking Greek to one another in what sounded like a heated argument. The recording only whetted the Mallones' appetite. They brought in another psychic, Leta Berecek, who wanted to see what automatic writing would uncover.

With her eyes closed, the right-handed Berecek held a pen in her left hand and let it wander across a sheet of paper. As she wrote in her trance, a candle near her began to expand and then exploded, spraying wax through the air like molten confetti. Berecek came out of her trance and read what she had written.

"I am James Garfield," Berecek read to the Mallones. "If you need proof, look at the candle. I am unhappy because so-called friends had me murdered." Mr. Mallone had a flash of inspiration. He brought out one of the completed crossword puzzles and compared the handwriting to that of Berecek's note. It was identical.

James Garfield, the nation's 20th president, had indeed once been a resident of the house. He had studied at the Western Reserve Eclectic Institute from 1851 to 1854. To support himself, he worked as the school's janitor; two years later, fresh from Williams College, Garfield returned to the Eclectic Institute to serve as an instructor in classical languages. When he became principal of the school just a year later, Garfield moved into the house that the Mallones would buy over a century later.

When Garfield first moved into the home, he met Almeda Booth, a woman with almost masculine features. Many described the domineering and headstrong woman as handsome and whispered that she had fallen in love with the future president. Unfortunately for Booth, Garfield was involved with

The family of James Garfield and wife Lucretia

Lucretia Rudolph, a classmate of his when he studied at the Eclectic Institute. She was far from stunning; in fact, she was frail and plagued with a variety of respiratory ailments, but she was intelligent and shared Garfield's thirst for knowledge. The two were married in 1858 but it seemed as if Almeda Booth wasn't willing to accept the union; sadly for Lucretia, Garfield may have encouraged her. While there is no evidence to support what might have been Garfield's infidelity, Booth and Garfield were seen in each other's company often after his marriage, and by some accounts Garfield and his wife feuded often—a situation that was only exasperated by their son's early death.

When the Mallones learned of their home's history, they realized that what had begun so many years ago had yet to be completed. The spirits that psychics Ed and Lorraine Warren had encountered were none other than Lucretia Rudolph and Almeda Booth, the former still lamenting her failing marriage, the latter still reveling as a result. Both Garfield and his wife were fluent in Greek. Perhaps their tape recording had inadvertently captured one of the many arguments the couple had had as their marriage disintegrated. Mrs. Mallone suddenly understood where the cigar smoke came from. In life, Garfield had smoked cigars, and as his spirit had been resurrected, so too, it seems, had his old habits. Pam, who had experienced an unusual amount of paranormal activity in her bedroom, learned that she slept in what had once been the Garfields' master bedroom.

The Mallones' concern was whether or not the spirits wanted to share the house that they so clearly felt they still occupied. They needn't have worried. The Garfields had been close with Marcia Henry's family and both were used to sharing living space with others. The house had been, after all, a boarding house. Marcia Henry had promised to return and she kept her word. Garfield, meanwhile, is believed to have come back to the one place where he'd once felt truly happy; it was an attempt to ameliorate his anger towards close friends whom he felt responsible for his assassination. (He was killed on July 2, 1881, in a Washington railroad station when Charles J. Guiteau shot him.) As for the other women, they stand as not-so-living proof that there are feuds not even death can mediate. The Mallones' dream house had become a kind of living museum, and the family happily welcomed its transformation.

Sutherland Place
PLACENTIA BAY, NEWFOUNDLAND

It was late. Jane (the names are fictionalized in this account) wanted nothing more than to get into the bed she shared with her boyfriend and drift off to sleep, cradled in his arms. She would wake him, whisper good night in his ear and then they would both drift into blissful slumber. Smiling, Jane unlocked the apartment door and pushed her way in. Moonlight that managed to peek its way between the drawn blinds lit the apartment dimly, as Jane found her way to the lamp she knew was just off to her right. The lamplight was soft, bathing the room in its warm glow. Jane beamed. John, her boyfriend, had actually cleaned the kitchen and done a half-decent job of it. She took off her coat and hung it on the door. It was good to be home.

She began walking towards the bedroom, but stopped abruptly in mid-stride. There, seated on the couch in the living room with her back towards Jane, was a woman. Jane felt a surge of panic and anger, and ran into the bedroom where she roused her boyfriend from sleep.

"Who is she?" she hissed into his ear. John, foggy with sleep and disoriented by the light, could only mumble incoherently.

"Wake up," Jane insisted, "and tell me who she is." John was still confused, not because he'd been woken up, but because the question made no sense to him.

"What?" he asked. "What are you talking about? What woman?"

"The woman in the living room," Jane said through clenched teeth.

"Are you drunk?" John could only stare at his girlfriend and wonder if the woman he loved was slightly crazy. "There's no woman in the living room."

"But there is," Jane insisted. "I saw her, clear as day, sitting on the couch."

"Jane, I swear to you, there is no one else in this apartment but you and me."

"Well, you go tell that to the woman in the living room. She's there."

"Fine. If it'll make you happy, you and I will go out there and you'll see."

They went to the living room, where Jane was shocked to discover the woman was gone. She was positive she had seen a woman sitting on the couch. She had even toyed with the idea of approaching her and asking her what she was doing there. So how was it that she now found herself staring at an empty couch? The woman, whoever she was, had vanished. For a moment, Jane thought that the woman might have left while she was inside waking John, but a quick examination of the windows and door revealed that they were all locked up tight from the inside. Whoever the woman had been, she apparently had the ability to walk through solid matter.

What Jane had seen and experienced was nothing other than a ghost. It was the latest in a line of inexplicable events connected with Sutherland Place in St. John's, Newfoundland. Jane didn't live in Sutherland Place, but there were theories that suggested that whatever it was that lingered in Sutherland had somehow managed to migrate into the neighboring building. Jane was not alone in what she had witnessed. Those in Sutherland Place had seen the very same spirit.

William Pitts built Sutherland Place in 1883. It was a grand Renaissance-Revival mansion constructed along King's Bridge Road. Pitts never lived a day in the house; he died before its completion, so his son, James S. Pitts, wearily took up residence. The house was far too big for one man to occupy so James rented parts of it out. For years, the distinguished Outerbridge family were his tenants. In 1892, Sir Leonard Outerbridge, later Newfoundland's second lieutenant-governor, watched from a top-floor bedroom window in Sutherland Place as the city of St. John's burned in the Great Fire. Sir Edgar Hickman bought the house in 1924 and planned to use it as an apartment building. It was around that time that the house's legend is said to originate.

English and French troops had battled for control of the continent for eight years in the conflict known as the French-Indian Wars. Throughout the conflict, King's Bridge Road had been a strategic route, crucial for the delivery of supplies from Portugal Coves and other ports to the British garrisons stationed at Fort William. Command of St. John's repeatedly shifted from the French to the English. Many battles were fought along King's Bridge Road and many young men lost their lives trying to protect or attack the city.

In 1924, tenants of Sir Edgar Hickman's new apartment building discovered that the changes Hickman had made to convert the mansion into an apartment must have roused something from deep within the earth and awakened a long-dormant spirit. Seen walking the property by a number of witnesses was the faceless apparition of a man dressed in military clothing, the style of which hadn't been seen outside a museum for close to two centuries. Because of his dress, the specter is believed to be that of a soldier who lost his life in one of the many battles that raged across the former battlefield. His face is never seen, hidden as it is beneath the high turned-up collars of his overcoat. Those who have seen him time and time again have become immune to the fear that most feel when they first see him. In fact, they have become comfortable enough with the soldier to christen him Peter Paul.

Peter Paul is not malicious; he seems content to roam the grounds where he sacrificed his life for his country. Surely everything he sees now must be a great mystery, since formerly barren land has given way to the technologies and advances of the 21st century. He must marvel at the world around him, taking great comfort in seeing people live the life that he was denied. Unfortunately, the unknown soldier is alone in his good intentions.

There is another apparition here, twisted and cruel. Her origins are unknown, but not long after another series of renovations at Sutherland Place had been finished in 1998, she began assaulting its tenants. One of them, Maureen, fled her apartment. Unsure of where to go for help, Maureen didn't know what to do. Her apartment was haunted—of that she was sure—but if she went to the authorities, they might not take her claims seriously. In desperation, Maureen turned to the Paranormal Society of the North Atlantic for help in determining what exactly had taken hold of her life.

First, she described to the society what had happened. Maureen had moved into Sutherland Place shortly after its renovations; by the second week of April, she had moved out of the building for good. For the time being, she was staying at a friend's house, terrified of going back to the apartment that to her seemed possessed with the spirit of something utterly unholy. Living there had placed both her emotional and physical health in peril. From the moment she moved in, she sensed that something was wrong. Anxiety and panic overtook her mind and she was at a frantic loss to explain why. Sleep escaped her as she sat in bed all night consumed by confusion. Still, she didn't want to abandon the building; she never thought that it might be the apartment that had been causing her so much grief. It's only a building, after all.

But then, one day, while talking to a friend on her phone, Maureen felt the strangest sensation. She felt as if she was being rocked back and forth, like a baby in a cradle, and realized with sudden and shocking clarity that her sofa was the cause. She leapt off the possessed piece of furniture and watched with a mixture of revulsion and fascination as the sofa continued to rock, front to back, until it slowly came to a halt. Maureen thought maybe it was a tremor of some sort, but had to discard that theory when she couldn't help but notice that nothing else in the room was moving, not even the glass of water set on a coffee table that was just mere feet away from the sofa. Something was astir in her apartment, but Maureen had little idea as to who or what it could be.

Maureen's desire to leave was strengthened the day the ghost attacked her. There is no elevator inside Sutherland Place, so to reach and to leave her apartment, Maureen had to climb and descend flights of stairs. One morning as she walked down the stairs, she felt, on her back, a push. Not expecting to be attacked in an empty stairwell, Maureen tumbled down the six steps to the first floor, tearing her new pair of pants. When asked whether or not she had been in a hurry and perhaps she had fallen because she missed a step or because she was wearing improper footwear, Maureen insisted that she hadn't been in any hurry and that she had been wearing sneakers. She remained convinced that someone or something had pushed her and that whatever had rocked her sofa was intent on doing her bodily harm. The Paranormal Society of the North Atlantic was intrigued and decided to investigate.

In the course of its investigation, the society learned that Maureen was not alone. There were other victims, all women. One of them dreamt that she was being pursued and woke up, bathed in sweat, pulse racing. The dream had been frighteningly vivid and the woman sat in bed, telling herself over and over again that it was just a nightmare, that there was nothing after her.

Imagine her terror, then, when she saw a figure walk through her bedroom wall and stop at the foot of her bed. Gripped by terror, she screamed, but the apparition—a withered old woman with long hair that seemed to disappear into her clothing—just continued to stare. The woman left the room as quickly as her legs could carry her and she sought refuge with her roommate.

The Paranormal Society of the North Atlantic visited Sutherland Place on April 10, 1998. They took some photos, noted that the room was unusually silent and then left for a half hour while they left a tape recorder running. Their pictures revealed nothing out of the ordinary, but when they played their tape back, the heavy silence that had seemed so overwhelmingly oppressive when they had walked the apartment appeared to have abated. On their tape was the sound of something, described variously as "two knocks on a wooden surface," "a washing machine in a spin cycle" and "a train." Yet the identity of the Sutherland Place ghost remains a mystery.

The results of the investigation were of little comfort to Maureen, who decided that she'd had enough encounters with the spirit. She moved out of her apartment the very day that she was pushed down the stairs, refusing to return to the building except to retrieve her belongings. Certainly there are those who question whether or not the events that took place in early April 1998 ever happened. For Maureen, her ripped pair of pants is proof that she encountered Sutherland's demon—the woman dressed in black.

3

Haunted
by History

H istorical societies and preservationists go to great lengths to restore houses to exact period details. But with some historic homes, preservationists find assistance coming from the least likely of sources: the spirits of those individuals they mean to honor and memorialize. How much more authentic could a historic home be if it is still inhabited by its most famous resident? The phantom footsteps and fleeting apparitions of a historic ghost provide an immediacy that historical interpreters dressed in costumes can only approximate.

Irving House
NEW WESTMINSTER, BRITISH COLUMBIA

Royal Engineer Colonel Richard Clement Moody founded the oldest city in western Canada in 1859. Queen Victoria, recalling her fondness for a London neighborhood, named the fledgling settlement New Westminster and proclaimed it the capital of British Columbia. Its location atop a hill where two branches of the Fraser River meet gave the city a strategic advantage against attacks and an economic edge as a gateway to the Cariboo Wagon Road that led to the Gold Rush. But by the middle of the 1860s, the rush had faded and New Westminster saw its prosperity diminish as a result. Victoria was made the regional capital and those seeking their fortunes in New Westminster would have to resort to other plans.

William Irving first arrived in New Westminster in 1859 from Oregon. He never left. His ghost haunts the Irving House, a residence built for him by the Royal Engineers in 1864. It is fitting that he remains there still, for he was one of those few who enjoyed prosperity even as New Westminster suffered through the bust of the gold rush. Irving, after all, came to British Columbia not to mine gold, but to mine the water.

Born in Scotland in 1816, Irving was destined for a life at sea. He sailed to Boston when he was just 15. Ten years later, he had become a captain and in 1849 he arrived in the Oregon Territory. The thick forests of Portland provided Irving with ready and plentiful fuel for the steamboats he planned to run along the Willamette and Columbia rivers. He prospered, but Irving was eager for new challenges and a market he could dominate.

In 1859, the steamboat industry in the Lower Fraser River valley was still in its infancy, providing Irving with a perfect opportunity. With his knowledge and experience, the waterways would be his. He established a navigation company operating a fleet of paddlewheel steamboats on both the Fraser River and on Harrison Lake; in the process, he constructed the very first steamer ever made in British Columbia. After he sold the company in 1862, he used the profits to open Pioneer Line so he could run boats on the Fraser between New Westminster and Yale. Irving succeeded and dominated, earning himself the nickname "King of the River."

The king reigned from a 14-room mansion. The home was built from redwood timber from California and hand-forged nails. Wallpaper was imported from Europe and holly bushes accented its green clapboard exterior. The latter were brought from Scotland to honor Irving's coat of arms, an armored fist grasping a sprig of holly. It was here where Captain William Irving, the head of an unrivaled steamboat empire, passed away in 1872 in a second-floor bedroom. New Westminster mourned his loss, the death of one whose "purse was always at the disposal of any one in need, and [whose] generosity was unrestricted by class, faith, or nationality…He knew of no distinction in his bounty and was a true gentleman in the true sense of the term." Irving loved the city and New Westminster loved its king right back.

In 1981, the Irving House was the first structure in New Westminster to receive municipal heritage status. Today, the city runs it as a historic center dedicated to illustrating the mid-19th century as well as showcasing the life of one of its beloved adopted sons. It is decorated with period furniture, accented by personal artifacts of the Irving family and enhanced by Irving's own ghost.

Strange noises are heard throughout the building, often in rooms that are for the most part empty. The walls appear to shiver in the dining room, while guests who visit the upstairs den report that the trophy heads of a moose and caribou turn to follow their movements. The bed in the captain's bedroom, moreover, will sometimes indent, looking as if someone were asleep in it. Although no one is there, an invisible voice sometimes speaks. As visitors approach the bed, Captain John Irving has been known to startle the unsuspecting by yelling out "Say my name!" Apparently his highness still expects respect in the afterlife. Why should he not?

Guibourd-Valle House
STE. GENEVIEVE, MISSOURI

Jules Valle lay in bed, with gauze and tape covering the socket from which one of his eyes had been removed just days earlier. The pain had subsided and he was beginning to regain his senses. Or so he thought. As he lay there, trying to adjust to the world through one eye, he was overwhelmed with a sensation that he was being watched. Perhaps his wife had come in while he'd been sleeping (as she usually did), so she could watch him from a chair across the room.

But then, just as he was about to turn to greet his wife, three heads obscured his view of the bedroom ceiling. He sat back with a start, wondering if he really had made as much as progress as he believed. But then he became calm.

Somehow the three faces beaming down at him assuaged his doubts about his sanity and soothed his fears about their identities. Jules then noticed something quite odd, a sight that would forever haunt his memory. Unlike most men, these three had no lower bodies. They were just torsos, arms and heads that hovered above the ground.

When he first moved into his vertical log house in Ste. Genevieve, Missouri, Jules had heard that something unnatural lurked inside. He had never himself witnessed anything that would lend support to the idea. Yet for months his wife had told stories about hearing footsteps creaking across her floorboards in otherwise empty rooms. In addition, their dog Jamie had been behaving strangely of late, growling and sometimes cowering in front of empty space. It wasn't as if Jules considered his wife a crackpot, but he wanted to see things for himself. As he lay in his bed, finding warmth and compassion in the three pairs of eyes staring at him, he suddenly realized the stories were true.

Jules had always believed that when he encountered a spirit he'd be frightened. Yet all the three disembodied ghosts did was nod, smile and utter sentiments he recognized as Spanish, as if offering both their best wishes for a speedy recovery and hopes for a long and blissful existence. On his deathbed ten years later, all Jules thought of were the three faces smiling down upon him and his dear wife, Anne-Marie.

Many thought Anne-Marie was a little foolish to continue living in the haunted home by herself. But she knew, despite never having seen them, that the three spirits that provided her husband with such comfort and peace would only have her best interests at heart. Besides, she didn't want to abandon

The historic Guibourd-Valle House in Ste. Genevieve, Missouri

the home in which she and her husband had spent so many blissful years.

Walking the halls of the empty house brought Anne-Marie joy and comfort. Everywhere she looked she would see the memory of something wonderful. So she stayed, watching with concern and slight amusement when her dog cowered in fear, shaking and shivering until he was able to get outside and escape whatever presence he sensed. Upon her death, she willed the historic property to the Foundation for Restoration of Ste. Genevieve so that the structure could be preserved as a memorial, both to its rich past and to her beloved husband. The home, now a museum and tour house, bears the names of two men, Guibourd and Valle, the first and last families to call the historic building home.

The Guibourd-Valle House was built in 1806 by French-man Jacques Dubreuil Guibourd on land he had been granted through a Spanish land grant. The vertical log house that he built must have been a vast improvement over the keg in which he had been smuggled to America—a necessary meas-ure after a slave uprising in Haiti threatened his life.

Landing in Philadelphia, Guibourd searched for Frenchmen or Creoles, people with whom he shared a culture and a lan-guage. When he landed, the port was teeming with Frenchmen recently arrived from Ste. Genevieve, who had come to Philadelphia on horseback to collect supplies. They agreed to take Guibourd with them back to Ste. Genevieve, which, despite being in Missouri, was the most Creole of towns. It would suit Guibourd perfectly.

Not long after his arrival, Guibourd married Ursule Barbeau and eventually produced four sons. He later built himself a new home, his previous one having grown too small for his burgeoning brood. The house, as it stands today, still retains most of its original framing and great Norman trusses—the enduring legacy of Guibourd's impec-cable craftsmanship.

When the Valles bought the house in the 1930s, Elizabeth Hens, a close friend of Anne-Marie's, came to visit. She immediately felt the presence of Spanish men. Indeed, while the Spanish held Ste. Genevieve for some years (before the French reacquired it), the Guibourd house was used as a meeting place for Spanish soldiers. Built by a Frenchman, haunted by Spaniards and now owned by Americans, Guibourd-Valle is the history of Ste. Genevieve writ small. And like any great history, the house has its mysteries. Who the Spaniards were remains unclear, as does

Inexplicable crashing sounds continue to disturb the living at Guibourd-Valle House.

the identity of the spirits that frightened Anne-Marie one March evening.

Anne-Marie awoke to what sounded like someone tearing apart her late husband's room. Crashes rattled her windows and the floors shook under the weight of what sounded like furniture being torn apart. Pictures and lamps were being smashed, and Anne-Marie could only wonder what was taking place in the room. The house was locked, so it couldn't have been burglars bent on theft. Even if they were thieves, what did they hope to steal after destroying everything of value?

Anne-Marie waited for the din to die down, but it persisted for ten more minutes. "I have a temper," Anne-Marie told ghost hunter Susy Smith, "and when it is aroused, I'm not afraid of the Devil." At the end of her patience, Anne-Marie sat up in bed and declared that the spirits would not frighten her; they would not scare her into leaving. The noises stopped almost immediately.

When she went to examine the room the following morning, everything was as it had been, untouched and preserved since the day her husband died. And so it has remained since Anne-Marie died and stipulated that the house and all its furnishings be used as a memorial. Preserved as a museum, the house is still home to the three Spanish spirits and some more besides. Perhaps sensing that Anne-Marie has left the house, the unknown energies responsible for the crashing sounds from her husband's bedroom have returned. When the room is investigated, of course, everything appears untouched. And everything, once again, is as it should be in the Guibourd-Valle House.

Chingle Hall
GOOSNARGH, ENGLAND

With the passage of the Act of Supremacy, which named the king the head of the Church of England, Henry VIII thus severed all ties with the Roman Catholic Church. The breach was motivated by Henry's wish to divorce Katharine of Aragon, and Pope Clement VII's unwillingness to fulfill that desire. Henry VIII's decision spawned a wave of terror, as a number of prominent churchmen and laymen were executed without mercy under the Act of Treason. Catholics were asked to take the Oath of Supremacy, recognizing Henry's place at the head of the Church of England. Those who didn't found, to their dismay, that the formerly enlightened Henry was now cruel and indifferent. Those who would not bend to the king's will were suppressed.

Henry ushered in an age in which Catholics were considered heretics and traitors; for centuries, hundreds would suffer from this association. Chingle Hall in the north of England remains particularly connected to Henry's reign of terror, making it quite possibly the most haunted house in the country.

Constructed in the 13th century, Chingle Hall was one of 5300 moated manors built in Britain for the aristocracy and the church. Its first resident was a knight, Adam de Singleton. The Singletons instigated the most peculiar chapter in the history of Chingle Hall. How exactly Eleanor de Singleton was descended from Adam is unclear, but most agree she fell out of favor with the family and suffered as a result. The girl was confined to her bedroom from age eight until her death (natural or otherwise) at 20. Even though her death took place centuries ago, she, along with John Wall, continues to call Chingle Hall home.

Not long after she was buried, people walking through her room were overcome with tremendous feelings of sadness and desperation. Others reported that the room smelled strongly of lavender even when empty. Still others had seen and actually heard Eleanor. The stories about Eleanor's room still circulate today as visitors continue to encounter Eleanor's ghost. If they don't run into her, then there is a good chance they will at least experience something strange. It is estimated that as many as 21 ghosts now haunt Chingle Hall.

When Henry VIII outlawed Catholicism, Chingle Hall became an impromptu church for those unwilling to convert. The home had a chapel and a Witches' Window, where which a candle was lit to let people know it was safe to approach. The original iron doorknocker was shaped like a "Y," the three points signifying the Holy Trinity. Those on the run because of their religious beliefs knew that to touch this knocker was to find safe haven for at least a little while. The Singleton family was Catholic and so were the Walls, who inherited the house after the Singletons moved on. Families continued to gather at Chingle Hall for secret masses, and it was here that John Wall was born in 1620.

As a practicing Roman Catholic priest, Wall refused to take the Oath of Supremacy. For his defiance he was arrested. In 1679, he was hanged, then drawn and quartered. His body and limbs were buried at St. Oswald's church, but it's rumored that French nuns smuggled his head to France as a religious relic. Eventually, Wall's head made it back to its birthplace and has remained there, along with his spirit, ever since.

Chingle Hall's most famous ghost has been seen walking outside a second-floor window, even though the window is 12 feet above the ground. Knock on a wall three times after saying "Jesus Christ" and John Wall will respond in kind. Other ghost monks have been seen praying in a downstairs room and walking the garden and south lawn. When renovations were made on the home, the removal of a large flagstone uncovered a hiding place, adding to those already found in the chimney and ceiling beams. These spaces hid religious vestments that are obviously not the only items to have survived the passage of time.

Elsewhere, a ghost cat still walks the main staircase. And although a stone bridge replaced Chingle Hall's drawbridge in the 16th century, people have reported that they can still hear, every now and then, the drawbridge opening and closing. White lightning and blue flashes periodically illuminate darkened rooms. In the kitchen, a ghost likes to break plates and stack pots and pans up to the ceiling. Once, two people were touring the kitchen when a wooden plaque floated off of the wall, traveled through the air to the middle of the room before dropping ever so lightly onto the floor.

Bonnie Singleton Richards, a direct descendant Adam de Singleton, was born in Portland, Oregon, but has returned on multiple occasions to Chingle Hall. Once, while she was taking a photograph of a room, she saw a doorway in the lens, but when she looked at the area again without the lens, she saw nothing. When she asked a guide about the experience, she was told that there had indeed once been a doorway there that led to a secret hiding room for priests.

Writing on the BBC's website, Bonnie recalled another incident. She had been invited to spend the night at the home and was sleeping soundly until something began brushing against her neck. She described the sensation as feeling "like a feather being passed back and forth over the back of my neck." At breakfast the next morning, she learned that the spirits of Chingle Hall were fond of touching people.

For those who lived in the house, the strange only got stranger. In 1968, footsteps and a loud knocking woke up two sleeping boys. When they opened their eyes, a strange light moving its way across the wall transfixed them. The light had the shape and form of a hand. It disappeared soon after. Margaret Howarth, a former resident, was haunted by doors opening and closing on their own, phantom footsteps and—strangest of all—spontaneous combustion.

Howarth noticed smoke billowing from the exposed wooden beams that run the length of the ceiling. Firemen came on the scene and were puzzled to discover that the fire had started from within the beams themselves. An investigation into the beams' history revealed that they were covered in strange markings and probably came from an old Viking longboat salvaged for use in the home's construction. What connection the beams may have with spontaneous combustion isn't clear, but the results have only deepened the mystery.

Chingle Hall isn't willing to give up its secrets just yet; it has resisted explanations for centuries now. While the identities of its most famous spirits have been uncovered, a host of others, such as the praying monks, may remain forever unknown.

Sprague Mansion
CRANSTON, RHODE ISLAND

In Cranston, Rhode Island, one cannot mention the name Sprague without conjuring up images of a time when the largely rural community, whose existence was once based upon agriculture, was the capital of an industrial empire whose reach stretched as far north as Maine and as far south as North Carolina. The Spragues' influence and affluence had no precedent in Cranston, and no one since has come close to equaling it. For three generations, the Spragues were big players whose successes in the textile industry translated into important political victories.

Those days are but shadows now, as the empire fell into ruin years ago. And were it not for the Cranston Historical Society, the most visible symbol of the Spragues' power, a grand and opulent mansion at 1351 Cranston Street might have been lost forever. Saved in 1967, the home is on the National Register of Historic Places and remains the most recognizable structure in Cranston. Preserved within is a part of Cranston's rich history. Not only are the people of Rhode Island grateful, but so too are two spirits who still consider the Sprague Mansion their home.

The Sprague family opened Cranston Print Works in 1807 when William Sprague began running a cotton mill on the banks of the Pocasset River. As they began to see profits, William and his son William II reinvested the money back into the company, purchasing water-driven power looms that managed both to increase output and decrease costs. As their company flourished, the Spragues were able to spend their money on life's luxuries and not its necessities.

The original Sprague house had been built in 1790. It was expanded in the early 19th century and then again in 1864 when a huge addition was erected. The home now stood at two and a half stories, with 10 bays and a cupola from which the Spragues could survey all that they owned: orchards, vineyards and woodlands, not to mention Cranston Print Works, a miniature city with two villages of mill houses, a school, a community store, boarding houses, a post office and a bank. More than one dignitary luxuriated in its grandeur and sipped brandy from fine crystal in front of one of the many Italian marble fireplaces.

But wealth and power were not enough to thwart the cruel and indifferent hands of fate. Blessed in all aspects, William Sprague met with the most pedestrian of ends in 1836. Dining one night on a supper of fish, William failed to pick out a fishbone from a forkful of food. The bone lodged itself in his throat and when doctors attempted to remove the obstruction surgically, William Sprague died.

Control of his empire passed to his two sons, William II and Amasa. Both had been elected to the state legislature, and it was decided that for the sake of the company, Amasa would devote a majority of his time to their father's work while William II would tend to matters political. Over seven years, son William saw his political star ascend. He filled various offices, including state governor and U.S. senator.

An untimely death struck the Spragues once again. In December 1864, policemen were summoned to Cranston Street where a body, beaten and bludgeoned almost beyond recognition, had been found along the road, just a short

William Sprague II, the former owner of a notoriously haunted mansion in Cranston, Rhode Island

distance from the Sprague Mansion. While the face was bruised and bloodied, authorities still recognized enough of its mangled features to see that another of Cranston's Spragues had met an unfortunate and tragic end. Someone had beaten Amasa to death shortly after he had left his mansion to travel to Johnston. A powerful man, Amasa had created many enemies through the exertion of his influence. Detectives theorized that a man, John Gordon, who had been denied a liquor licence because of Amasa, had ambushed the man he deemed responsible for his failures. He exacted a most terrible and heinous revenge. Gordon was tried for his crimes, found guilty and then hanged. But evidence later revealed that Gordon had not been guilty. This gross miscarriage of justice led the state of Rhode Island to abolish capital punishment. As for Amasa's real killer, he never was found.

With a heavy heart and a broken spirit, William II abandoned the Senate and returned to Cranston to take over the family business. Amasa's children did honor to their father. One son became governor while another became a brigadier general in the Union Army and later a U.S. senator. But despite the best efforts of the Spragues to sustain the company's prosperity, fortunes declined after the close of the Civil War. The once great family saw its wealth dwindle away to almost nothing. Bit by bit, the empire was dismantled. First went the vineyards and the horse track. Then the holdings in other business ventures. Necessity then dictated that the Sprague Mansion be sold as well. The empire had fallen.

The mansion went through a number of reincarnations, including a boarding house and a foreman's residence. Its demolition was scheduled for 1967 but the Cranston Historical Society intervened, acquiring the property and restoring it to its previous splendor. They opened it to the public and might have been pleased to learn that spirits— one of whom is suspected to be Amasa—have returned to the mansion.

A ghost was first seen in Sprague Mansion walking down the grand mahogany staircase. Not long after, residents found that a good night's sleep was a precious luxury. More

Sprague Mansion, built in 1790 and expanded twice

often than not, an invisible force would wake slumbering residents when it flung their blankets and sheets off the bed. The room that was subject to the strangest and most intense phenomena was the Doll Room, so named for the collection of porcelain dolls that stare blankly across the room. People hear footsteps, yet when they turn to see who is approaching, they only see the dolls staring back at them. Lights turn themselves on and off while a gray mist floats above it all. In the wine cellar, cold spots chill the bodies and souls of the unsuspecting.

Curiosity led to a séance in the mansion to determine who exactly was haunting the home. When a Ouija board began to rock, violently spelling out, "My land! My land! My land!" the participants became frightened and stopped the séance. Although the session was cut short, the researchers did uncover the identities of the spirits. One is a butler who worked in the house during the late 19th century, a disgruntled employee who had expected an inheritance upon his employer's death but received nothing. It seems his goal is to disturb the living because of the perceived slight. He is most likely the one responsible for disappearing blankets.

Amasa, on the other hand, continues to walk the staircase of the house from which he controlled his family's empire. His is a mournful spirit, desperate to understand both his fate and the Sprague family's decline. It must be of great comfort to him that Cranston has seen fit to honor the memory of their most famous sons through the preservation of what was once the jewel in the Sprague family crown.

Sturdivant Hall
SELMA, ALABAMA

When Mr. and Mrs. Robert Sturdivant donated $50,000 to the community of Selma, they wanted their money to help develop a showcase for their collection of antiques. Today, Sturdivant Hall bears their name because of their generosity. But there's more on display in the house than the Sturdivants' stellar collection. The house is known as much for its unique Southern furniture as it is for the continued presence of a man who passed away in 1867. John McGee Parkman may have only lived in the house for two years, but if anyone were to still call Sturdivant home, it would be Parkman.

Sturdivant Hall was built on a lot that Edward T. Watts bought for $1830 at a public sale. He hired Thomas Helm Lee, a cousin of Confederate general Robert E. Lee, to design and construct the Neoclassical mansion. After a year, Watts had his home erected at a cost of $69,000. Watts lived there with his wife Louisa for 12 years before he decided to sell the property.

Elias Parkman arrived in Selma in 1817. His son John was born in 1838. John turned out to be a prodigy of sorts, a hard-working and dedicated industrialist who started out selling dry goods and progressed from clerk to bookkeeper to bank teller to cashier. In 1866, he was named president of the First National Bank of Selma and entrusted with capital totaling over $100,000. Two years earlier, he had bought the Watts property for $65,000. Just 28 years old, John seemed as close to happiness as one could get. How could he have known that within a year he would lose everything he had spent his life working for?

Shortly after he was named bank president, a man came to meet John at his office. The man presented himself as General Wager Swayne, commander of the Federal troops stationed in Selma. He announced that John was being placed under arrest and that the bank and its assets were now under his control. John could only stare incredulously at the general. He believed that he had always acted with integrity and honesty, as did the people who knew him.

General Swayne was dismayed to learn that John, like so many others at commercial houses, had used bank capital to speculate on cotton. The investment proved unwise. While many others who had been guilty of the same act did not go to jail, the glaring difference in John's case was that the United States government had large deposits of money in the bank. John had lost these, making his arrest a necessity. Protest as they might, John's family could not convince Swayne of John's innocence. He was arrested, convicted and thrown into a Confederate prison at Cahaba.

But John wasn't without his allies. Family members and friends conspired to free him and, on the appointed night, arrived at Cahaba. A guard was bribed to leave John's cell door open. He slipped out under the cover of darkness, made his way past the prison walls and was almost at the river when a guard in a watchtower spotted the fleeing prisoner. He gave John a warning, but it went unheeded. John was so close to the riverboat destined for Selma that he refused to surrender. Freedom, he felt, was within his grasp.

The guard fired once, twice. John fell into the river, dead. His wife, with no income, was forced to sell the home, at a huge loss, for $12,000. John Parkham was buried in Live Oak Cemetery—or at least his body was. The same can't be said of his spirit. His family might have moved on, but John wasn't quite ready to abandon his Selma house.

The Gillmans bought the home and it remained in their family until 1957, when the city of Selma bought the home for $75,000, $50,000 of which came from the late Robert Sturdivant, whose will had provided for the creation of a museum in Selma. One wonders now if Sturdivant had meant a haunted museum.

John returned to what is now Sturdivant Hall and has haunted the building for years. His apparition has been seen looking out from the cupola at the top of the house. Visitors and volunteers at the museum report that his presence can be felt in an upstairs bedroom as well as in the downstairs parlor.

One time, concerned neighbors summoned the police to the property when they saw windows and doors opening and closing on their own. Officers forced their way into the building only to discover that nothing was amiss. All the doors and windows were securely fastened and, most curious of all, the building was empty. Firefighters were just as puzzled when they were called out to Sturdivant Hall because more than a few concerned citizens had seen smoke billowing out from the upstairs windows. There might have been smoke, but there was definitely no fire, leaving a squad of confused firefighters.

Pat Tate has written about her experiences in Sturdivant Hall. On numerous occasions she has heard phantom footsteps moving across the second floor of the house. She has seen doors open and close on their own and has found beds in disarray when, just moments earlier, they were neatly made. Whenever the doors open, Tate greets John Parkham, saying "Good evening."

The mansion was the venue for a ball that followed a re-creation of the Battle of Selma. People were stationed at the staircases to make sure that no one mistakenly wandered upstairs, which was restricted to museum staff. Tate noticed that one of the people had abandoned his post. When he returned, Tate questioned him as to where he had gone. The guard claimed that he had gone upstairs to investigate three reports of children looking out the window. He found nothing except empty rooms.

During another incident, an exterminator fled from the house. He had been spraying the rooms upstairs when he felt a strange sensation—a feeling that someone was pushing him from behind. He raced down the stairs and out of the house, pledging never to return again. In other corners of the house, witnesses have seen rocking chairs rock on their own, while a group of children were startled when a painting appeared to leap off an easel and shatter into a hundred pieces. The children were not nearly as rattled as one might have thought; after all, they knew that it was just John Parkham making his presence felt.

Sturdivant Hall is listed on the National Register of Historic Places. Its collection of period furniture, portraits, silver, dolls and toys recreate the antebellum South, allowing visitors to step back in time. The home is still regarded as one of the most unique and beautiful homes in the Southeast. John Parkham must surely agree.

Baleroy Mansion
PHILADELPHIA, PENNSYLVANIA

In Chestnut Hill, Pennsylvania, a historic district of cobblestone streets and grand homes noted for both architecture and history, sits Baleroy Mansion. Since 1923, generation after generation of the Easby family has lived in the 30-room mansion outside Philadelphia. The house was so dear and close to the heart of some family members that they continue to call Baleroy home. Although the manifestations are not normal men and women, the long-dead Easby relations are undeniably human in spirit. Their personalities, their quirks and their preferences are all still intact. For the Easbys living in Baleroy now, the continued presence of the dearly departed must surely be a comfort.

Yet there are those who claim that parts of the house are cursed, that death will surely follow those who choose to tempt their fates. A blue fog—what researchers and ghost hunters might call an ectoplasmic mist—anticipates the appearance of Amanda. Her past is unknown and how she came to haunt Baleroy is a mystery. But if the rumors are to be believed, Amanda's origins are the least of anyone's concerns. Over the years, three deaths have been attributed to her. After appearing before each person, she used her wiles to lure each one to sit in a particular chair in George Meade Easby's study. After getting up from the chair, one might have only a short time to live—maybe a day or two or perhaps a month. Regardless, the minute these individuals sat in the chair, they were marked for death. The only questions were when and how they would die.

Paul Kimmons, a fervent non-believer in the paranormal, was convinced that all the reports he'd heard about
Baleroy Mansion and its curse were nothing but wild and
unproven allegations that he was determined to undermine.
Accompanied by a psychic, Kimmons visited the Baleroy. His
life was changed forever.

While walking by the staircase, Kimmons' doubts vanished when Amanda's ghost suddenly materialized on the
steps. He could only stare at the apparition. The accompanying psychic remembers that Kimmons became visibly
agitated. The vision unsettled him. Days later, the psychic
received a phone call from Kimmons. He pleaded for help,
for some direction. Amanda's spirit was haunting him.
Everywhere he went, there she was. He couldn't escape her,
not even in the sanctuary of his own bedroom. Fear and
terror became his perpetual companions. He met the psychic
again at the Baleroy, determined this time to end his suffering. Weary and exhausted, Kimmons sat down in the chair in
Easby's study to rest. He died a month later.

The psychic who saw Kimmons through his ordeals
understood how one might link the curse with the man's
death, but she believes that there was no curse. Since his
death, she has sensed his presence many times at the
mansion and she feels no remorse or bitterness on Kimmons'
part. She only feels his warmth. The psychic believes that
Amanda's presence has been misunderstood. She appears
not to snuff out life, but to ease the transition from life into
death. No minion of the grim reaper, she is a guide.

The intentions of the other spirits here do not create as
much mystery or confusion. They return out of love and
compassion. The two other spirits of Baleroy, after all, are

dear to the home's current owner, George Meade Easby. They are the ghosts of his mother, Henrietta, and brother, Steven. It is fitting that the past takes on such a life in Baleroy Mansion. After all, Easby has dedicated his life to collecting fine art and preserving the treasures of his home. He has in his collection sterling silver used by the signers of the Declaration of Independence, as well as a cannonball taken from the fields of Gettysburg—the very one that killed his great-grandfather, Union General George Meade. The artifacts tie Easby to the past, uniting the living with the dead with tangibles that stir the soul. Among them is the paranormal presence of his brother, Steven, who died when he was very young.

When Easby and his brother were children, the courtyard fountain proved fascinating. Like Narcissus, the children were captivated by their reflections; they could spend the better part of an hour watching these mirror images. One day, Easby peered down into the water and, as is to be expected, he saw his face staring back at him. Next to him was Steven, doing the same. But when Easby looked into his little brother's reflection, he saw not his sibling's face, but a skull. He recoiled in horror, casting a quick glance again at the water. All he saw now was his brother's beaming face. The image filled Easby with dread—a sensation that only found release when Steven died a short time later. Steven now turned to haunting the Baleroy.

While working near the courtyard fountain, restoration specialists have reportedly seen a head of tousled blond hair appear in an upstairs window. As they watched the child, the workers gasped when the blond head disappeared. One of the workers who witnessed the phenomenon was so petrified he left the same day, swearing he would never return. He never did.

Another worker in the basement heard what sounded like a child's voice repeating his name over and over again. Puzzled, the worker was convinced that his co-workers were having a laugh at his expense. Yet when he questioned them about it, they had no idea what he was talking about. In fact, they had all been on the third floor of the house, much too far away to sit by a staircase and say a name over and over again.

On another occasion, a loud crash interrupted a dinner party on the terrace. Easby was shocked to learn that a painting of Steven had flown 15 feet from the wall it once hung on and crashed to the ground. The nail from which it hung was still protruding from the wall and the wire that held the painting up was fully intact. But if everyone at the house was seated on the terrace, how did the portrait end up where it did? Easby attributed the accident to his brother.

He did the same when a visiting minister was hit in the side of the head by a copper pot that appeared to fly across the room, thrown by unseen hands. The minister left the house soon after and never came back. Like any child, Steven craved attention. When a reporter came by to report on the phenomenon, Steven couldn't resist pulling the man's tape recorder from his hand. The reporter watched in awe as he saw his tape recorder fly in an arc from his hand, guided by invisible forces. He was so taken aback that he stepped outside to sit on the terrace, a shot of whisky his sole companion.

Easby himself often encounters not only Steven, but also his mother, Henrietta. She announces her presence with loud footsteps and repeated knocks. Easby was in bed one evening when he felt someone else get in after him. He was alone and, as he turned on the light to greet his intruder, he wondered how anyone could have gotten into his home without first tripping one of the sensors on his security system. But the light revealed just an empty bedroom and Easby contented himself with the thought that perhaps he had only imagined the sounds. He had just gone back to sleep when something grabbed his arm and began to pinch and squeeze his skin. When he awoke the next morning, he could only wonder whether it had all actually happened. One look at his arm told him all he needed to know; there were blue and gray bruises from the pinches.

Henrietta's spirit contacted a psychic once, repeatedly whispering the words "Longfellow" and "children's hour." The psychic was positive that she was trying to communicate a message to her but she couldn't be sure until later that night. Walking through the study, the psychic noticed that one of Easby's many books had been pulled out slightly from a shelf. The psychic pulled it down and turned the book to a page bookmarked by an envelope. On the marked page was a poem written by Henry Wadsworth Longfellow entitled *Children's Hour*. Written on the envelope, in the floral curves of what could only be Henrietta's handwriting, was a message: "To my son Meade in the event of my death." The envelope was empty and when the psychic told Easby the story, he gasped. *Children's Hour* had been Henrietta's favorite poem; with its words, she had often lulled her cradled babe to sleep. Easby read the poem aloud, his heart swelling with the memory of his dead mother.

The events of that night marked the beginning of a "spirited" period during which Henrietta began revealing the location of a number of hidden items throughout Baleroy.

Among other things, there were silver candlesticks and a tattered flag General Meade had captured during the Battle of Gettysburg. Henrietta also led her son to a letter that apparently revealed that great-great-grandfather Richard Meade had loaned the United States $5 million years ago to cover the debts tied to the American takeover of Florida. If such a note and claim were true, Easby was owed millions from the federal government. The claim has never been substantively proven, but one supposes that Henrietta was only interested in ushering her son into a past of which he knew little. It was a means of preserving a legacy, of establishing a concrete connection between past and present. It is also a means of preserving the Baleroy, the house that the Easbys—both dead and alive—still call home.

Nottingham Castle
NOTTINGHAM, ENGLAND

As the site of both personal and national tragedy, it's no wonder that the remains of Nottingham Castle are among England's most haunted places. Of the original castle, which has been destroyed twice, all that remains are parts of its gatehouse, its foundation and a network of tunnels that cut their way through the sandstone bluff upon which the castle was built. No living person has resided in these ruins for centuries. It's a different matter altogether for the dead.

Edward I died in 1307, leaving the English crown in the possession of his son, Edward II. Almost immediately, Edward set in motion the forces that would topple him from power.

The Gate House at Nottingham Castle, one of England's most haunted places

The new king foolishly alienated the barons, who were crucial for replenishing the royal coffers depleted by his father's invasions of Scotland. The barons, in turn, imposed their will through an ordinance that obliged Edward II to maintain laws chosen by them. Robert the Bruce's decisive victory over Edward's troops in a 1314 battle further eroded any support or confidence Edward might have once had. But just as it appeared that Edward was at his weakest, he struck back.

Thomas of Lancaster led the barons. By 1315, he had effective control of the country, but he proved far less able when asked to wield power. He was incompetent and lazy, content to rely on existing laws to check Edward. It was a shortsighted mistake that allowed Edward to march against his cousin in 1322, resulting in the defeat of Lancaster at Boroughbridge. Lancaster and his supporters were summarily executed; it appeared that Edward II had recaptured control. Looking without, Edward could see no threat. He should have looked within.

His queen, Isabella, had long ago decided that Edward was not the stuff of kings. She considered him weak-willed, ignorant and corrupt—a man whose homosexuality left her alienated and alone. Isabella's meeting with Roger Mortimer, was more than just a simple twist of fate. He appreciated Isabella for the woman she was and he had even attempted to seize the throne of England in 1323. The two came together in France, where Isabella was working as an envoy to her brother, French king Charles IV, and where Mortimer had been exiled after his failure to wrest the crown from Edward. Isabella fell in love and they began plotting to overthrow her husband.

With German and Dutch mercenaries, the conspirators landed in England in 1326 and began attacking countryside, capturing those nobles still loyal to the crown. Edward II was imprisoned in Berkeley Castle. While no one knows exactly what happened, Edward died the most grisly of deaths there, probably at Mortimer's request. Isabella's son, Edward, took up the crown, but his mother and lover wielded all its power. Mortimer's ambitions were boundless; it was clear to all that his eye was fixed firmly on the crown and all who stood between him and the monarchy was young Edward. Edward III was a puppet. It was a role he would soon tire of playing.

In 1330, Isabella and Mortimer were staying at Nottingham Castle when Edward decided to act. Accompanied by a handpicked troop of soldiers, Edward gained access to the castle through the tunnels running through its sandstone foundation. Edward captured Mortimer in the bedroom, then placed his father's murderer in cuffs while Isabella watched helplessly. As Edward led Mortimer away, Isabella is believed to have said, "Fair son, have pity on the gentle Mortimer."

Edward did not listen. Mortimer was executed a month later for treason. Like many before him, he was hanged then drawn and quartered. His remains were left to rot on Tyburn Gate. But something of the traitor survived. He still returns to Nottingham Castle where he haunts the passageways beneath what is now called Mortimer's Hole. His capture proved more than he could bear; he guards the tunnel zealously now, forever trying to foil his captors.

Isabella, meanwhile, spent the rest of her life confined to Castle Rising in Norfolk. The woman known as the She-Wolf of France died there in 1358, alone, insane and hysterical. Centuries later, just after World War I, American soldiers were staying at the Jerusalem Inn, located next to Nottingham Castle. One evening, the soldiers were surprised when the screams of a Frenchwoman rent the air. They heard the same phrase uttered again and again, its repetition further entrenching the words in memory. An inn worker was asked to translate what they had heard and to offer an explanation for what had happened. The soldiers were told that they had heard the pleas of Queen Isabella, asking Edward II to "have

Nottingham Castle no longer serves as a royal residence, but long-dead former occupants still roam its halls.

pity on gentle Mortimer." The soldiers had been witness to what many before and many since have experienced— Isabella's ghostly cries from the night her machinations were brought to an end.

Hers are not the only cries heard at Nottingham Castle. Edward II was not the only monarch to stir resentment towards the crown among the baronial class. Even earlier, in the 13th century, King John had lost possessions in

Underground caves add to the mysterious allure of Nottingham Castle.

Normandy, Anjou, Maine and parts of Poitou to France. His reputation in tatters, John resolved to restore his legacy by intensifying his efforts. The escalation in war meant escalation in cost. For the barons who bore the brunt of John's increased taxes, the situation had become untenable. They acted, but failed in an attempt to remove John from the throne. The king's wrath was boundless. In retaliation, he took 28 sons of traitorous Welsh noblemen and had them held captive in Nottingham Castle.

He kept his hostages alive for a little while before they were led up the castle's ramparts and hanged for the sins of their fathers. To this day, their screams for mercy can still be heard up on the ramparts. Those living around the castle reported for years that the ghosts of these boys would appear in their homes, lost and confused.

Although Nottingham Castle no longer serves as an official royal residence, for a select few it remains home. Their presence is a lasting reminder of how power can pervert the human soul.

Haliburton House
WINDSOR, NOVA SCOTIA

The first Canadian international bestseller was *The Clockmaker*, a compilation of stories that had previously been published in the newspaper *The Nova Scotian*. The willingness of the public to buy a volume of predominantly recycled material speaks to its popularity. First published in 1836, *The Clockmaker*'s success spawned a series of books, all revolving around its comic protagonist, Sam Slick. The character's popularity pleased its creator, Thomas Chandler Haliburton. Slick was a mask, a means for Haliburton to express strongly held progressive views that clashed with those of the conservative ruling elite of which he was a part. Sam Slick found affinity with the public on both sides of the Atlantic, spurring publishers to release multiple editions and others to pirate copies. Haliburton, for his part, continued to write from his home in Windsor, Nova Scotia.

Writers are peculiar creatures. Subject to fleeting moments of inspiration, they develop habits meant to ease the creative process. For Haliburton, he was most comfortable writing in the elegant wood villa he had built in 1834 in Windsor. This 15-room home overlooked a sprawling estate of 40 acres and is preserved as a museum that showcases life in the 19th century. Some of Haliburton's own artifacts are on display and, if rumors are to be believed, so too is Haliburton himself.

Haliburton was born into the Windsor aristocracy. He was the scion of a respected judge and the grandson of a successful lawyer. He was expected to exceed, or at the very least match, the achievements of his forebears. The young Haliburton did not disappoint. After graduating from King's College in 1815, he began studying law under his father's tutelage. In 1819, he was called to the bar, and, after a brief sojourn to England where he married Louisa Neville, a captain's daughter, Haliburton began practicing law at Annapolis Royal. Amiable and charismatic, Haliburton found himself ranking among the influential and powerful. With such support, an election to a seat in the House of Assembly in 1826 seemed only fitting for the socially minded lawyer. It must have frustrated Haliburton, then, when he found himself unable to act freely upon his liberal progressive instincts.

Dedicated first to family, Haliburton reined in his instincts. The ruling elite was conservative and resistant to change. Haliburton could risk his family's reputation and standing if he spoke out against what he perceived to be social inequities. It was then that he decided that he would create the quick-witted and quick-tongued Sam Slick. Through Slick, Haliburton was able to offer up his challenge to politics. Slick was Haliburton's Trojan Horse; his views had the potential to alienate, but dressed in Slick's humor and outrageous behavior, they were not nearly as offensive.

Slick the Yankee clock peddler first appeared in *The Nova Scotian* in 1835, recurring in 21 separate installments before Haliburton's publisher and friend, Joseph Howe, compiled the stories into one volume. Accompanied by Howe, Haliburton toured England and Europe in 1836 as a literary celebrity. Public response prompted him to release two more books, one in 1838 and another in 1840. Haliburton had found professional success and, more importantly, his reputation among the conservatives was intact. A judge on the Inferior Court of Common Pleas since 1829, Haliburton was elevated to Nova Scotia's Supreme Court in 1841, making him the youngest judge on the bench. Sadly, Haliburton's private life provided a single note of tragedy. Wife Louisa died the same year.

Haliburton recovered from the shock of her death and continued to serve on the bench and to write from his home. He retired in 1856 and moved to London, away from the only home had he ever known. But as in Windsor, he dedicated himself to public service, winning a seat on the British House of Commons in 1858. After a lengthy illness, Windsor's favorite son, Thomas Chandler Haliburton, died in 1865 and was buried in Middlesex, England, far from the land of his birth.

In life, Haliburton used his influence and position to make changes. He had a hand in the development of both the Avon River Bridge and what is now known as the Windsor-Halifax Railway. Some view him as the "Father of American Humor," whose creation, Sam Slick, popularized phrases such as "he drank like a fish," "you can't get blood out of a stone" and "facts are stranger than fiction." By some accounts, he is North America's most frequently quoted author. His appeal

The ghost of Thomas Chandler Haliburton is said to emerge from a secret panel and walk around his former home.

and influence was obvious even in the 19th century. Oxford University awarded Haliburton an honorary degree in literature, the first colonial to be granted one.

Haliburton's heart was Nova Scotian, and even in England Windsor was never far from his thoughts. It's not at all surprising, then, that after death the man has returned to his home. Haliburton House Museum is alive with his spirit. Haliburton's ghost is said to emerge from a secret panel in the reception hall to walk around his home before returning to the room from which he appeared. Those who have seen him say that the ghost always walks the grounds with a smile. Windsor honors Haliburton each year with Sam Slick Days, recognizing his contributions to literature and the city he loved.

4
Lady
of the House

T he spirits in this section reflect women's roles over the centuries. As you can probably imagine, this group couldn't be more diverse. Wealthy and powerful women are represented, as are simple servants with quiet but touching stories. Several of the ghosts revisit the living as a reminder of tragic love, while others prove that not all wandering women are innocent as they first appear. What they all share is an insistent desire to return and to have their stories survive in the minds and hearts of the living. Many visitors to their former homes can still sense their feelings of loss, longing and melancholy.

Liberty Hall
FRANKFORT, KENTUCKY

Generations of the Brown family lived in Liberty Hall, the home that John Brown, one of Kentucky's first senators, built in 1800. The home was completed four years after Brown bought several acres of land overlooking the Kentucky River. It quickly became known as one of the finest Federal-style homes in the state. Visitors who passed through its halls were culled from the American elite, including President James Monroe, Colonel Zachary Taylor and Colonel Andrew Jackson. The last of the Browns to live in the grand mansion was Mary Mason Scott, who passed away in 1934. She willed the house to her brother, John Matthew Scott.

Unfortunately, John Matthew's life and work were both situated in Louisville, and he was reluctant to be burdened with the responsibility of caring for the property and all its buildings. He sold the estate to a non-profit organization of concerned Frankfort citizens who sought to preserve the home as a museum. And so, for the first time in 134 years, Liberty Hall would not serve as a residence for a Brown.

But that statement isn't entirely true. In truth, Liberty Hall has continued to serve as a home of sorts for one Brown family member in particular. John Brown's wife had an aunt who died at the home, and fate has conspired to keep her in Liberty Hall—an ironic name considering the aunt appears to enjoy no liberty at all. Even now, over a century after her death, Margaret Varick still walks the home's halls.

Margaret lived in Liberty Hall for only three days before she died of a heart attack. She had made an 800-mile journey

The Gray Lady of Liberty Hall in Frankfort, Kentucky, often tucks people into bed.

by horse and carriage from New York City at the request of her niece. Mrs. Brown had lost her mother at an early age, so responsibility for her care had fallen to the aunt. Naturally, when one of the Brown children passed away in infancy, Mrs. Brown turned to the woman who had seen her through her deepest loss. Margaret, whose health was already precarious, could not refuse the woman she had come to love as a daughter.

The journey exacerbated an already fragile heart. Margaret was buried in the family plot by the gardens and, for a while, it seemed as if she had found peace. But when the cemetery was moved to a larger one in Frankfort, the caretakers entrusted with the task managed to misplace Margaret's body. Far from New York and removed from eternal peace, Margaret's spirit was restless.

Her first appearance took place during a wedding. Brown's grandson was a little disturbed to learn from his bride that she had seen a ghost while getting dressed for the wedding in the bedroom in which Margaret had died. She was alone, so she was quite flabbergasted when she saw a woman dressed in gray walk through one of the bedroom walls, across the floor in front of her and through another wall. The figure looked all too familiar; the bride soon realized that she recognized the spirit from family photographs. The ghost bore a striking resemblance to Margaret Varick.

When Mary Mason Scott lived in the house, she saw Margaret on numerous occasions. Mary remembered how vivid her great aunt's face had appeared to her when she awoke one evening to see the apparition, once again dressed in gray, standing above her. Over breakfast, friends and guests staying over at the house would share stories of how they had each woken throughout the night to find a woman in gray tucking them into their beds. And so Margaret Varick, beloved aunt and surrogate mother in life, became the Gray Lady, helpful spirit and generous ghost in death. Rarely were people frightened by her appearance. Those familiar with the ghost acknowledge that Margaret is just there to help. She has been known to do errands around the house, making beds in the morning and mending clothes in the afternoon.

One time, a guest was taking a bath. She had already immersed herself in the tub when she realized that she'd forgotten to close the bathroom door. Slightly irritated, she stood up only to see the door close on its own. Sometimes Margaret does more. Because she came to Liberty Hall to comfort her niece, she has been known to soothe constitutions worn by anxiety and worry.

Taken over by Liberty Hall, Inc., Liberty Hall found new life as a historic site. One of its employees was in an office, staring wistfully at a music box given to her by an old boyfriend. She reached for the gift, longing to hear its twinkly music, then stopped abruptly. The air was swelling with the tune of the music box. She stared at the box, finding affinity and warmth in the nostalgia ushered in by the melody. She acknowledged the Gray Lady's presence with a small smile and a nod.

Passersby often see the Gray Lady standing by a window as they walk by the house. A professor, eager to test his hypothesis that the image was created not by a ghost but by the reflection of moonlight, spent six weeks in the mansion without finding any evidence to support his theory. Instead, he was roused from slumber one evening by a gentle touch on his shoulder. When he looked up, he saw Margaret smiling down upon him, waving. He came to the conclusion that perhaps there was a spirit inhabiting Liberty Hall. At the very least he was now certain that Margaret Varick was still around. The other two spirits he wasn't so sure about.

Two additional apparitions roam Liberty Hall: a Spanish opera singer and a soldier from the War of 1812.

Besides Margaret, two other apparitions haunt Liberty Hall. One is a Spanish opera singer who was abducted from the gardens of the house one night during a party. She was never seen again, except on hot and humid nights when her ghost, with mouth wide open, eyes a study in terror, runs through the garden, forever trying to escape her kidnappers. The other spirit is represented by the ethereal echo of a soldier who fought and died in the War of 1812. Before he was sent to the front, he fell in love with one of Brown's cousins. He returns to Liberty Hall to peer into the house from outside, hoping to catch a glimpse of his lost love. One supposes he'll have to settle for the company of the Gray Lady, Liberty Hall's most famous and celebrated resident.

Wedderburn Mansion
NARRAGANSETT, RHODE ISLAND

The story of Wedderburn Mansion is about love—unrequited love, to be exact. It is a tale of desperation, of the darkest impulses lurking within the heart and the inability to resist them. Even to this day, the story's tragic conclusion reverberates through Wedderburn Mansion in the form of a grieving ghost.

The four-story, white clapboard house was built by a wealthy sea captain, Japhet Wedderburn. But the house was far too big for a bachelor to take care of by himself. An extra set of hands was required for the maintenance of the house. He took out an ad in the local paper, asking for a dedicated housekeeper. She would have to be accustomed to being alone, since Wedderburn spent months, sometimes years, away from Narragansett. The captain's true mistress was the ocean, specifically the waters of Asia where he plied his trade. Whoever became his housekeeper would have full run of the mansion in Wedderburn's absence.

Wedderburn finally settled on Huldy Craddock. Of those who had come to his home seeking the post, she alone had demonstrated the devotion required of the job. He was quite impressed with the woman's skills and liked the look of her; she was heavy-set and strong. There was little doubt in Wedderburn's mind that his house would be in good hands with Huldy.

When told the news of her hiring, Huldy was ecstatic, but not for reasons Wedderburn might have suspected. Yes, room and board were welcome to Huldy but she wanted the job for reasons far more personal. Ever since she first caught a glimpse of Wedderburn as he disembarked from his ship, with his sun-bleached hair radiant like a halo and his sun-dappled skin bronzed like a Greek god, she knew that she wanted not only to love him, but also to possess him. In Wedderburn's posting, Huldy saw an opportunity so sublime and perfect that she had no choice but to seize the chance. And so she did. She moved into Wedderburn's house and set to work.

Huldy's plan had one minor problem. Wedderburn didn't find Huldy attractive in the least. Unlike the waters he navigated, the sea captain was rather shallow. When he looked at Huldy, all he saw was a frumpy, plain and unattractive servant. Wedderburn preferred his woman petite and exotic; he remained blissfully unaware of Huldy's intentions.

Huldy soon realized that Wedderburn would never love her in return. Outside of her job, it was clear that Wedderburn barely even knew that she existed. This realization was met with bitterness and anger at first as the days passed her disappointment faded. She came to accept her position but taking consolation in being the only constant woman in Wedderburn's life. Gone at sea for months at a time, Wedderburn had no time for a relationship with any woman. Huldy consoled herself with the fact that if she wasn't to possess Wedderburn, at least no other woman would either. And so it was until one fateful day when Huldy went down to the pier to greet Wedderburn upon his return from another voyage.

There he was, as always, smiling broadly. He had a bag in one hand, but what was that in the other? He was holding the hand of a woman, leading her off his ship and onto the gangplank. Huldy gasped. There, draped on Wedderburn's arm, was the most beautiful woman she'd ever seen around the ports of Narragansett. She was small, with delicate features, tanned skin and dark, long, lustrous hair. In her hair was a tortoise shell comb and she wore a black lace mantilla. She was everything Huldy was not. Staring at her in the sunlight, Huldy felt her world shudder. And when Wedderburn greeted Huldy and introduced the woman as Dona Mercedes Wedderburn, his *wife*, her world shook. But she hid her disappointment well.

Dona and her husband settled into married life at the mansion. But after just a few months, Wedderburn became restless, tired both of domestic life and his wife. He began taking his ship out again, sailing the seas for weeks at a time, leaving Huldy and Dona behind in the mansion to wallow in their self-pity. Huldy lamented Wedderburn's marriage, while Dona longed to return to see her family once again. The beginning of the end came when Wedderburn announced that he was leaving for two years, unaccompanied by his wife. Dona begged him not to leave, or at least to take her back home. He refused his wife on both counts and set sail.

Wedderburn returned two years later and certainly couldn't have missed Dona terribly. She had disappeared, and when he asked Huldy what happened, she said that Dona, having given in to homesickness and despair, sailed for Spain months earlier. Wedderburn accepted the news with a simple shrug. Lonely as he was in Narragansett, he'd often found more than enough company on the high seas to satisfy his loneliness. Dona's absence was treated as if he had come home to the news that his white clapboard house had been repainted. He simply stopped off in his mansion for a short while, bid a farewell to Huldy and once again set off to sail the oceans, this time for good. Wedderburn suffered a heart attack and died. His body was returned to Narragansett where he was buried.

Over the next 50 years, varied occupants and visitors of Wedderburn were startled by the strangest of things. The event didn't take place every day, but when it did, it was always at dusk, when day and night are one. Standing in the front room, witnesses were startled when a child-like woman, dressed in black with a tortoise shell comb in her hair and a black lace mantilla on her shoulders, appeared in front of them as if from nowhere. She approached the window, looked out across the great expanse of water before her with longing, her solemn visage a study in loneliness. When people approached her, she disappeared. For years, few had any idea who the apparition might be. Dona had kept to herself during her time in Narragansett; Huldy had been her only companion, so few recognized the ghost's mantilla and comb as Dona's favorite accessories.

It wasn't until 1925 that the ghost's identity became clear. That year, an organization had bought the home with the hopes of using it as a summer retreat for poor children. An examination of the home revealed that renovations would be needed. The hearthstone in the fireplace was badly cracked and would need to be replaced. Workmen were brought in to remove the cracked hearthstone and repair the damage of years past. But when the hearthstone was removed, the workmen made a gruesome discovery. There, underneath the fireplace, was a crude wooden coffin. And while the body inside had decayed and rotted away, leaving just skeletal remains, two items had been preserved: a tortoise shell comb and a black lace mantilla.

Dona hadn't sailed back to Spain after all. There are suspicions concerning Huldy's role in Dona's death, but how she might have done it remains unknown. One suspects that Huldy's love became a poison that polluted her soul. It corrupted her, leading her to eliminate the one obstacle in her path to lifelong happiness with Japhet Wedderburn. Ironically, of course, Wedderburn never loved Dona. His true love was and always had been the high seas. As for Dona Mercedes Wedderburn, she continues to stare out the windows of Wedderburn Mansion, eternally hoping for someone to whisk her away to her home and family.

The Luna-Otero Mansion
LOS LUNAS, NEW MEXICO

Los Lunas means "where the Lunas live." And considering that the spirits haunting the Luna-Otero Mansion in Albuquerque, New Mexico, tend to be various relations and descendants of the once powerful and socially prominent Luna-Oteros, the name couldn't be more fitting.

Los Lunas is a community of 20,000 people nestled among the cottonwoods lining the banks of the Rio Grande River. It is a place where horses are still used for transportation and where a rural lifestyle is cherished. Time is savored here in Los Lunas and so too is its past. And nowhere is its pull felt more strongly than in the Luna-Oteros, a mansion built in the days before the railroad had united east and west, north and south. The property is a remnant of the days when two powerful Spanish families dominated and ruled Los Lunas.

In 1692, the Lunas, headed by Domingo de Luna, arrived in New Mexico to take possession of land granted to him by the King of Spain. The Oteros, with Don Pedro Otero as their patriarch, arrived a short time later to seize their own parcel of land. As the years passed, the Lunas and Oteros prospered through the acquisition of both land and livestock. In short order, both had amassed fortunes rivaled only by the other. Socially and politically, the Lunas and Oteros dominated. By the late 19th century, the two did what prominent families the world over had done for years: they united their clans in marriage. Solomon Luna married Adelaida Otero and Manuel Otero married Eloisa Luna, creating the Luna-Otero

The Atchison, Topeka and Santa Fe Railroad was forced to alter its route to accommodate the powerful Luna family.

dynasty. United, their power was such that the Santa Fe Railroad was forced to bend to their will.

In 1880, the Santa Fe Railroad was slowly making its way through New Mexico. Engineering plans called for the railroad to pass through Luna property. In order to secure the right of way, the railroad had to deal with the Lunas. An agreement was reached that ensured the construction of a grand mansion, built to the exacting specifications of Don

Antonio Jose Luna and his family, in exchange for the right of way. Don Antonio had taken a number of trips throughout the South and wanted a home that mirrored the grand and sweeping architectural styles he had seen as he had traveled from plantation to plantation. The railroad built him a grand mansion in the Southern colonial style, using adobe as its primary construction material.

Don Antonio spent little time in the mansion; he died just a year after its completion. But the building stayed in the family, passing to his oldest son, Tranquilino. But while serving in the Senate in Washington, Tranquilino fell ill and died, leaving the home in the hands of his younger brother, Solomon Lunas. After his death in the early 20th century, the home passed to a nephew, Eduardo Otero, and his wife, Josefita Manderfield Otero. By all accounts, Josefita was a beloved matriarch of the Otero family and Los Lunas in general. Known as Pepe by those who loved her, Josefita spent her days tending to her gardens and painting. She was a devoted philanthropist, contributing generously and selflessly to causes benefiting the wellbeing of Los Lunas. And it was under her care that the Luna-Otero Mansion underwent a series of renovations. Josefita Otero added a solarium, a front portico and ironwork that extended the property. Save for the ironwork, which has been scaled back, the house still bears the splendor of its days as the jewel in the Luna-Otero crown.

Power, unfortunately, is not permanent. By the 1970s, the mansion had become a relic, a memento of the past. As such, it was protected as a historical landmark so that Los Lunas need not forget those who had a hand in its creation. Still protected, the home is now a restaurant with patrons able to enjoy a meal in the opulence and splendor of days past. And if guests are fortunate enough, their stay might be graced by the grand dame of Luna-Otero herself, Josefita Manderfield Otero.

For as long as anyone can remember, Pepe has haunted Luna-Otero. Why would she ever leave? She had given so much both to the mansion and the community. Her elegant hand and eye transformed both. And so she has stayed, devoting her afterlife to her life's passions. Death has not changed her habits. When she appears, she is still dressed in the period finery of the 1920s and still frequenting the same rooms. Her apparition has been seen in what were once bedrooms on the second floor and an attic storeroom. More often than not, though, Pepe can be found at the top of the stairs in her favorite rocking chair.

A waitress at the Luna-Otero restaurant once saw Pepe rocking slowly back and forth. Concerned that someone had neglected who she thought was a customer, the waitress walked over to the chair. As she did, the figure, bracing herself against the chair's arms for support, began to rise from the seat. The waitress stopped and stared in complete bewilderment. As the stranger rose, her body appeared to dissolve until there was nothing left but an empty landing and chair. The waitress rubbed her eyes in disbelief. It wasn't until later in the evening when she mentioned the incident that she learned about Luna-Otero's permanent resident. Other witnesses have seen Pepe walking up and down the staircase and throughout the main dining room. She is said to have the look of a woman with a distinct sense of purpose and place—an aura and authority that removes all doubt as to who is truly the owner of the grand old building.

There is still one more spirit in the home. His origins are unknown but his appearance has fooled even the most dedicated hostesses. Once, a hostess noticed a sharply dressed man sitting on a sofa. His legs were crossed at the knees, while he watched the room with an air of amusement and contentment. Although he looked as if he had no need of anything, the hostess still felt compelled to ask another waitress why the handsome stranger hadn't yet been served. The waitress claimed that there was no handsome stranger. The hostess protested, saying there had to be, that she had just seen him sitting on that sofa. But when she turned her attention back to the sofa, she only saw the last wisps of the man fade into black. Who was he? His origins remain a mystery, but it seems as if Pepe is not starving for otherworldly attention in the Luna-Otero Mansion.

Stevenson House
MONTEREY, CALIFORNIA

The child didn't exactly see dead people. But he could sense their presence, and for one schoolteacher accompanying her students on a field trip, that was eerie enough. As the child walked through a historic home, his teacher was amazed as he began describing people and places from long ago. She didn't really believe he was speaking the truth. He was just indulging his suddenly overactive imagination, inspired by the presence of things he'd never seen before. In the nursery, he talked about feeling two children, infants deathly ill and fighting for their survival. Watching over both of them was

Robert Louis Stevenson (left), shown here with his family, stayed briefly at Stevenson House in Monterey, California.

their self-appointed guardian, a grandmother ready to fight for their lives. When the child moved into another bedroom, he saw, lying on the bed, a man gasping for air, whose chest heaved and surged with every breath and whose body rocked and rolled with each convulsing cough.

He described all these scenarios to his teacher, who nodded and smiled in amusement. But later a guide pulled her aside and asked her how the child knew so much about the house's history. The teacher hadn't a clue. As it happened, the child, far from exercising his imagination, was something of a clairvoyant. It was the only way to explain his accuracy; the child had never been to the home before. There was little chance that he could have had previous knowledge of the house's history. And according to the guide, the child was correct in his account of the history of Stevenson House in Monterey, California.

Stevenson House may have been named for writer Robert Louis Stevenson (he stayed there briefly in 1879), but it is not his spirit that is held responsible for most of the paranormal activity that takes place. The credit goes instead to the wife of a Swiss businessman, Manuela Girardin. The Girardins bought the adobe house built in the 1830s from Don Rafael Gonzales. They expanded it, opening up wings of the house to be used as a business, The French Hotel.

Robert Louis Stevenson, writer of classics such as *Treasure Island* and *Dr. Jekyll and Mr. Hyde*, stayed in the hotel during his pursuit of the married Fanny Van de Grift Osbourne. Upon meeting the American mother of two in a garden in the French tourist resort of Grez, he was immediately taken by her delicate features and long locks of sable hair. Osbourne was sketching at the time; Stevenson did not learn until later that she had been drawing him. Her return to California and her husband threatened to cleave Stevenson's heart in two, but he was determined not to let the woman who could be the greatest love of his life slip from his grasp. When he received a telegram revealing that Fanny's divorce was not yet a reality, Stevenson refused to sit idly by. He left Scotland for America, arriving in New York 11 days later. The journey took its toll on the young writer, whose weak chest and susceptibility to inclement weather were only aggravated by the cold raging rains of the Atlantic Ocean. When the ship docked at New York Harbor, a coughing, wheezing Stevenson disembarked and boarded the overland train for San Francisco. By the time he arrived in Monterey, Stevenson was violently ill. He checked himself into the French Hotel. It was December 1879.

The French Hotel was more charnel house than five-star accommodation at the time. Typhoid had arrived in Monterey, bringing illness and death. Manuela Girardin did all she could to keep her family from being touched by typhoid, but two of her young grandchildren had contracted the disease. She watched over them in the nursery while also tending to the bronchial afflictions of Stevenson. She left the running of the hotel to her husband, devoting herself instead to her grandchildren. In a peculiar twist of fate, Manuela contracted the disease herself and died soon after. Through her Herculean efforts, the grandchildren survived and Stevenson recovered. All remembered Manuela's compassion and dedication.

As for Stevenson, he wrote *Old Pacific Capital* while in Monterey and is said to have been inspired to write *Treasure Island* while walking along the Monterey Peninsula. Osbourne was finally able to secure her divorce, and within weeks Stevenson's father had wired him some money for a wedding. Stevenson wrote that his "marriage was the best move [he] ever made in [his] life." Most would agree; after the union, Stevenson's writing entered its golden period. Stevenson would later attribute his success to his marriage. He died in Samoa on December 3, 1894, at the age of 44.

As for the house in which he stayed, it changed hands over the years and was scheduled to be demolished until

A devoted grandmother is among the spirits at Stevenson House, named for the famous author.

Edith Van Antwerp and C. Tobin Clark raised the funds necessary to save it from destruction. The home was presented to California as a memorial and is now a part of Monterey State Historic Park. While Stevenson only spent a few months in the house, several rooms have been dedicated to displaying Stevenson memorabilia, such as first edition books, manuscripts, trinkets and other personal effects donated by family members. But in the nursery, during the first weeks of December, strange happenings suggest that the home reflects the influence not only Robert Louis Stevenson, but of Manuela Girardin as well.

There is a rocking chair in the nursery that rocks all by itself. Then the smell of carbolic acid, a common disinfectant in the 19th century, materializes out of nowhere and hangs heavily in the air, wrinkling the noses of confused visitors. The chair stops rocking and then a ghost in a long black gown with a high lace collar appears. She walks over to the children's bed in the nursery, gazing down lovingly at figures only she can see. Then she disappears, venturing back into the nothingness from which she came. Guides and those familiar with Stevenson House all agree that even in death, Manuela Girardin continues to nurse the ill, never once stopping to think about who might minister to her. Stevenson House may bear the writer's name and hold his furnishings, but its "spirit" is personified by the specter that appears every December to remind visitors of her sacrifice and dedication.

Captain Lord Mansion
KENNEBUNKPORT, MAINE

The Lord family left quite an impression on Kennebunkport. While the coastal retreat is noted today for being the summer home of former president George Bush and his wife Barbara, it was not always so. Many call Kennebunkport home, not just a weekend retreat. In fact, some believe there are ghosts who have inhabited Kennebunkport since the late 19th century. They haven't let death keep them from enjoying life on the coast. One of these is Phebe Lord, the wife of prominent shipbuilder Nathaniel Lord. Her home, built in 1812, is one of the grandest homes ever constructed along the beaches of Maine. With over 16 rooms, four stories, a magnificent four-story elliptical staircase and awe-inducing views of the carefully groomed lawns, it's not surprising that Phebe has had trouble leaving her home behind.

During the War of 1812, a British blockade of the northeastern Atlantic coast threatened to cripple the country. Trade came to a standstill as boats laden with goods were

unable to leave or enter the harbor. Kennebunkport's economy depended on this trade. Merchant and shipbuilder
Nathaniel Lord found himself with little work to do.
Fortunately, money wasn't an issue; just before the British
Navy barricaded the harbors, Lord had managed to obtain a
shipment of salt. In short supply because of the war, salt was
a valuable commodity and Lord profited from its sale. But he
was paying too much to employees who merely sat on the
piers and stared out at the ocean. Lord wanted nothing of the
sort. Blockade or not, he was going to put his men work.

When Lord married Phebe, her father gave his son-in-
law land at the head of the village green. This land was to
be the site of Lord's new house. He commissioned Maine
housewright Thomas Eaton, a man responsible for the
design and construction of magnificent Federal-style homes
throughout the northeast, to build a mansion fit for a man
of his class and standing. Eaton didn't disappoint. After a
frantic six months of construction, Lord had his house. The
most magnificent of its features was the rooftop cupola.
From here, the Lords were able to revel in the majesty and
breadth of the Atlantic Ocean. The cupola's inclusion in the
home's design was a nod to Kennebunkport's importance as
a port. A separate staircase was added to the home so that
expectant villagers could scan the waters for ships bearing
their loved ones. It was also where Phebe Lord would spend
many of her days, gazing out at the ocean with eyes tinged
with loss, tears trickling down her cheeks. The house, after
all, was not a home, but a memorial.

Despite all the money he expended on the home's construction, Nathaniel Lord had little time to enjoy the pleasures of his palace. His health had been flagging for some time

and in the afterglow of the mansion's completion, it became all too clear that his life was in jeopardy. Phebe did what she could, but his illness was beyond her ability to heal. She resigned herself to his inevitable death, watched her husband breathe his last, and then kissed him through the salt of her tears. Phebe lived out the rest of her days in the mansion that bore her husband's name, pacing the widow's walk.

After her death, the home was deeded to her son Daniel. He, in turn, left the house to his sister Susan and her husband Peter Clark. Their son Charles P. Clark inherited the home in the late 19th century and initiated most of the changes that have come to define both the Captain Lord Mansion and Kennebunkport. He installed the home's signature elliptical staircase and carried out extensive renovations throughout. Clark was also unhappy with his view of the Kennebunk River. He considered it obstructed by three houses, so, in a display of his power and influence, he had the houses moved. The move left a wide expanse of green space called the River Green—the perfect staging area for craft fairs and art shows, and the setting for the many gala events for which Clark was famous. But the parties had to end sometime, and when Clark died the home passed to his daughter Sally and her husband Edward Buckland. She lived in it until 1941, when her daughter Julia took up residence. Julia's death ended over a century of the Lords' presence in the house. The home became a boarding home for seniors and eventually a bed and breakfast, which it remains today.

But even as generations of Lords came and departed, one thing has remained constant in the mansion. One resident still lingers out on the widow's walk, pacing back and forth with hopes for her husband's return. Witnesses have seen this woman dressed in early 19th-century fashions, walking both the cupola as well as in the bedroom once known as the Wisteria. This is wholly appropriate, considering that "wisteria" translated means "remembrance of the dead." Phebe's continued presence in the Captain Lord Mansion ensures that few will ever forget the first lady of the house.

Phebe walks the staircase, the hallways and the widow's walk, appearing and disappearing as quickly as a wisp of smoke. The impression she leaves lingers for much longer. A newlywed couple was celebrating their union in the mansion. The bride, looking to freshen up, padded off quietly to the bathroom while her new husband flipped the channels of the television. Thoughts about the future were driven from his mind as soon as he heard his wife's shrieks from the bathroom. He jumped from the bed and flung open the bathroom door where he saw, standing in front of his wife, the ghost of a woman in a nightgown floating towards him. To his amazement, she passed right through him. Then the couple watched with mouths agape as the apparition slowly made its way across the bedroom, through the bed and then through the wall. Their honeymoon was memorable, although for reasons they might not have anticipated. Phebe Lord, devoted wife and suffering lover of Nathaniel Lord, has appeared many times in her home since her death, ensuring that those who come to this magnificently restored bed and breakfast may find their stay accompanied by paranormal encounter.

Ashton Villa
GALVESTON, TEXAS

The day was anything but ordinary. When the sun finally set in Galveston, Texas, on September 8, 1900, 6000 people lay dead and a third of the city had been leveled. Such was the work of the deadliest natural disaster to ever hit the United States; a hurricane attacked Galveston Island with winds beyond 120 mph and a tidal wave that rose like a malevolent hand, crashing upon the city with all the force that nature could muster.

It was an ignoble fate for a city that boasted the fourth-largest population in Texas. Galveston had reveled in its commercial prosperity and its billing as the "Wall Street of the Southwest." The city was the site of Texas' first bakery, first cotton compress, first gas lights, first opera house, first medical college and first school for nurses. Reconstruction after the disaster took years as Galveston went to great lengths to protect itself from such a catastrophe ever occurring again. Eventually a great seawall was completed in 1962, at the cost of $15 million dollars, while the entire city was raised 4 to 6 feet over 8 years. But one house remained where it had stood. Winds could not destroy it, waters could not carry it away.

Built of iron and brick, Ashton Villa is a grand three-story home with 13-inch thick brick walls, long elegant windows and graceful verandas topped with lintels made of cast iron. It's said that while the rest of Galveston fled in terror before the approaching storm, Ashton Villa's residents, the affluent Brown family, did not budge. They calmly opened the front

Some of the carnage wrought by a destructive hurricane in Galveston, Texas, on September 8, 1900; 6000 people perished in the disaster.

and back doors so that the waters could flow through unimpeded, leaving the house securely on its foundations.

One of the Browns' younger daughters spent the fateful day watching the floodwaters rise to the 10th step of the majestic staircase. She marveled at the river flowing through her house. Although the other homes were razed, Ashton Villa was not; the property came away untouched. Its one concession to nature was the filling of its basement with sand

and silt from the Gulf of Mexico, while the surrounding grounds were raised by 2 feet. The flood, however, is by no means the only interesting story surrounding the house and its past. To this day, Ashton Villa's fascinating ghost remains a powerful symbol of the family that first constructed the grand mansion on Broadway Street.

James Moreau Brown was a man of many interests, including banking and the railroad. But what created his prosperity was the wholesaling of hardware. By the late 1850s, Brown owned the largest hardware store west of the Mississippi. With his wealth he bought four lots at the corner of Broadway and 24th and began constructing a grand home as a showcase for his success. The resulting Italianate palace, which took four years to build, required the services of skilled European craftsmen and a small army of assistants. Upon its completion, Brown's wife, Rebecca Ashton Stoddart, christened the home Ashton Villa in honor of Lieutenant Isaac Ashton, an ancestral hero who had served with distinction in the Revolutionary War.

The house's crowning glory was the room known as the Gold Room, a lavish and ornate formal dining room designed with the elite of Galveston in mind. Such was its glory and splendor that both Union and Confederate generals claimed the mansion as their headquarters, depending, of course, on which army held the city. It's even said that the surrender of the Confederate forces of the southwest took place in the Gold Room. Yet for all its vaunted history, Ashton Villa is famous today for quite another reason. Although there are some claims to the contrary, Ashton Villa has often been called the most haunted house in the United States—a reputation earned through years of dedicated haunting by one Miss Bettie Brown.

Born in 1855, Bettie Brown was one of James Brown's many daughters. By all accounts she was at once the most beautiful and the least attainable. Fully aware of her charms and beauty, Bettie refused to curry the favor of one man alone. She was no one's prize to claim, and while her independence eventually alienated her from her father, she cannot be faulted for choosing to live her life on her own terms. Like Mother Nature, Bettie's was a will that could not be contained.

Bettie's position as the daughter of Galveston's royal family afforded her opportunities to indulge her every whim. Her youth was spent in carefree oblivion as she bought expensive gowns, traveled from one resort to another, collected art and furniture and broke the hearts of more than one optimistic suitor.

When her father died in 1895, Ashton Villa became hers. It was the perfect display case for the antiques, valuables and art she had collected throughout her travels. But lest one receive the impression that Bettie was a self-absorbed princess of privilege, it was she who helped with efforts, as part of the Women's Health Protective Association, to bury the dead, to distribute relief supplies and to rebuild the city after the Great Storm of 1900. Bettie never married, and until her death she never appeared to want for company. Her home was a social epicenter, the venue of choice for parties and dinners that raged late into the night. But in 1920 Bettie Brown died and a soul that few ever knew emerged. Death stripped away her carefully constructed facade of fierce independence to reveal a lonely soul.

After Bettie's death, the villa was sold to El Mina Shrine, who made minor adjustments to the property so it could be used as a business office. In 1968, El Mina Shrine put the

*Ashton Villa, which escaped harm during the hurricane, is home to the
forlorn, unloved spirit of former resident Bettie Brown.*

property up for sale. The house needed to find a buyer fast or
risk demolition. With public funding and private donations,
the Galveston Historical Foundation bought Ashton Villa,
restoring it to its previous splendor with the home's original
furnishings, art and valuables, most of which were collected

by Bettie Brown. It's fitting, then, that Bettie returned to the mansion that was a reflection of her former life.

There is little doubt that Bettie is the spirit haunting Ashton Villa. Whenever she is seen, most often on the mansion's grand central staircase, she is clad in a turquoise gown. Turquoise, as those familiar with Bettie well knew, was her favorite color. She still treasures her collection of antiques and is especially fond of an ornate chest from Asia. Its key lost long ago, the chest still locks and unlocks all on its own, to the great marvel and amazement of Ashton Villa's curators. The bed in what was once Bettie's bedroom refuses to stay made, its sheets and pillows crumpling and indenting as soon as they have been smoothed and straightened. A weekend manager, Lucie Testa, described in 1993 how she had turned off the ceiling fan atop the staircase only to return the next morning to find that the fan was still in operation. That event took place on February 18, 1991. Had Bettie been alive, she would have celebrated her 136th birthday on that day.

Most often, Bettie is seen in the Gold Room where she plays mournful dirges on the grand piano that is the room's centerpiece. Glamorous in life, Bettie has changed little in death. She sits at the keyboard, her long blonde hair piled high upon her head as ringlets of tresses cascade down her cheeks, the most immaculate of frames for her pristine beauty.

This vision greeted a caretaker who had crept into the moonlit room believing that someone had broken into the house. The moment his eyes fell upon the apparition, he knew that he was looking at no mere burglar; here was the grand dame of Ashton Villa in her full glory. In that instant, he knew that the stories he had heard were true. He crept carefully behind a Chinese screen to watch Bettie at the piano and then watched, transfixed, as another spirit—this one a man with dark curly hair and a beard—appeared from the shadows.

"It is foolish for any man to talk to you about marriage," the man said. "You couldn't really love anyone, for you are too absorbed in your own pleasures, your collections of meaningless objects and most of all your looks."

The caretaker watched in shock as Bettie wiped away her tears with a silk handkerchief. He knew that this was a side of Bettie that few had ever seen. Imperious and cavalier in life, Bettie was now all too human, as vulnerable and weak as any other living creature.

"Harrison, do you really believe this?" she asked, her voice broken and unsteady. "I won't listen to such hateful words."

The conversation was over. She turned back to the piano and began to play once again. Harrison turned and walked away, his form disappearing into the shadows from which he emerged. The creaking of the floorboards in his ears was all the caretaker had to reassure him that he hadn't imagined the entire exchange. Bettie continued to play but then stopped. She then stood up and approached a mirror, imploring the object to tell her who was the fairest of them all. As she stood watching her image in the glass, she faded away into nothingness, a woman unable to receive love or to love in return. Bettie's tragic fate is to wander Ashton Villa surrounded by the only things that she was ever capable of loving—stunning but lifeless objects.

Carleton House
SIERRA VISTA, ARIZONA

When Captain Samuel Marmaduke Whitside set up camp in the Huachuca Mountains, he might have done so with the hopes of establishing a fort. He could not have known that over a century later Fort Huachuca would be as well known for its tenure as a U.S. Army base as it is for a spirit that continues to linger in the halls of Carleton House. Countries have trembled before the might and power of the U.S. Army, but not Charlotte, the spirit who continues to appear before soldiers and officers with the same indignation and irritation as she has for years.

Carleton House was named after Brigadier General James H. Carleton, who led the California Column during the Civil War. Built in 1880, it was used as the fort hospital. Legend has it that a woman once gave birth there to a stillborn son. Without the money necessary for a proper burial, the woman, sickly and weak, was forced to stand by helplessly as the army buried the child in an unmarked grave somewhere on the property. Within days, the mother was dead too.

But eternal rest was not what she was sought. She returned to Carleton House, determined to find the body of her dead child. By all accounts, she has not been successful, for she has haunted the house from its days as a hospital through to its varied incarnations as officers' housing, officers' mess, post headquarters, school house and governor's retreat. Since the 1950s, Carleton House has been used once again as living quarters for officers stationed at Fort Huachuca, once the home of the famed Buffalo Soldiers of the 9th and 10th

Cavalry and now headquarters for the U.S. Army Information Systems Command, the Army Intelligence Center and School and the Electronic Proving Grounds. Charlotte has remained its one constant. Whenever something odd or perplexing happens in Carleton House, Charlotte is assumed to be the cause.

Charlotte first acquired her name when Brigadier General Roy Strom and his family lived in Carleton House during the 1980s. Strom was sure it wasn't her real name, but it seemed appropriate to give the entity haunting the house some personality. Charlotte seemed a fitting moniker for the ghostly apparition seen wearing a light-colored gown with ruffled edges.

The Stroms encountered Charlotte on their very first day in the house. Using one of the bedrooms for storage, the Stroms returned to the bedroom to retrieve some personal items. When they turned on the overhead lights, they were stunned to see that someone or something had emptied out all the boxes and strewn their contents all over the room. It was later discovered that the room had once been used as the hospital morgue. Perhaps Charlotte was looking through the boxes to see if she could glean any information about her child. The same night, as Mrs. Strom was placing clean towels in the linen closet, a white mist swallowed her up. Surrounded by the localized fog, Mrs. Strom felt none of the sensations usually experienced when walking through a mist. She was not cold or damp, just quiet with awe at the air swirling around her.

As the weeks passed, the Stroms couldn't help but wonder if they were an inconvenience to the ghost. Decorations they put up in the living room would be torn down—anything from posters to photographs would be found in piles on the floor. The doorbell would ring insistently, yet when answered, no one would be there. No matter how vigilant the family was, they never found anyone at the door. The problem became so persistent that the doorbell had to be disconnected. In one corner of the house, the air insists on remaining permanently cold, no matter how warm it is outside or how high the temperature is inside. The chandelier that hangs over the corner refuses to come on at night, but adamantly stays lit during the day. Hoping to curry the ghost's favor in some small way, Mrs. Strom christened the nook Charlotte's Corner.

Other families followed the Stroms' lead. They decorated the corner with a rocking chair and a doll, inviting Charlotte to relax whenever the search for her child grew too wearying. To their credit, Charlotte seems content. Her vaporous form, clad in the ruffled gown that few have worn since the late 19th century, has often been spotted in the rocking chair.

Charlotte's appearances have sometimes resulted in cases of mistaken identity. When one mother in the house saw a figure walking near the kitchen, she called out a good evening, thinking the form was her daughter. But the figure didn't return the greeting. And when she passed by her daughter's room, just moments later, she saw that her child was already in bed, sleeping peacefully. She realized that whoever she'd seen in the hallway couldn't have been her daughter.

The Koenigs, who lived in Carleton House before the Stroms, once received an irate phone call from a neighbor, who wanted to know what gave them the right to ignore her son. The angry mother told the Koenigs how her son had returned home earlier in the day and had asked her what he had done to wrong the family living in Carleton House. Although he had clearly seen a blonde-haired woman walking down the hall through the entrance window, no one answered the door when he knocked. The Koenigs laughed, explaining that it was all a simple understanding. They hadn't been home all day to answer any knocks at their door; what the son had obviously seen was Charlotte the ghost. In fact, the Koenigs' daughter Nancy had just seen the apparition days before.

After returning home from a date, Nancy approached her parents' bedroom to let her mother know that she was home, as she had promised. She then spotted a figure down at the end of the hall, dimly lit by a nightlight, who she assumed was her mother. She called out to the form and then went to bed. The next morning, Mrs. Koenig wanted to know why Nancy had broken a promise. Her daughter protested, claiming that she had indeed said good night when she got home.

"Don't you remember?" Nancy asked. "You were in the hallway."

Mrs. Koenig then understood. "Nancy, dear," she said, "you must have said good night to Charlotte."

There is a small room underneath the house. Not quite a cellar, it is more like a storage area for the house's water heater. It cannot be entered through the house; one must go through a door near the front and down a small series of steps to reach it. Repairing the heater has always proved difficult. Repairmen have been known to flee the room, not because of anything they might have seen or encountered, but because they are overwhelmed with a pervasive sense of dread. Psychics investigating the room have come to the conclusion that it exerts a force over individuals who are particularly sensitive to the world beyond ours. They also believe that there is a presence inside the room—that of a small child who could very well be Charlotte's baby. An excavation of the area would be quite impossible now, but one hopes that Charlotte finds peace soon.

5

Infamous
Abodes

The following stories cover haunted houses that have grown from local curiosities into nationally and sometimes internationally prominent paranormal meccas. Because these houses are associated with famous people, important events or unusual circumstances, many people are skeptical about the ghosts inside. The many versions of each story, moreover, suggest that perhaps no definitive version of the haunting exists. But one thing is certain—each fresh listening and interpretation seems to reveal something new. That is why the stories endure.

Windsor Castle
BERKSHIRE, ENGLAND

For a bunch of kids out looking for fun, the night was one that they would never forget not even if they tried. They would forever remember the time in 1962 when they encountered Herne the Hunter.

At the edge of a clearing in Berkshire, England, the group found a hunting horn. One blew on it and they continued walking. And then they stopped. Off in the distance, they could hear an answer to their call. It opened with a horn, its bright and clear tones cutting through the night. And then there was what sounded like a low rumble that rose in pitch with each passing moment. As the rumble got closer and louder, the youths finally realized that they were hearing the barking of many dogs. Punctuating it all was a thundering of hooves.

The group couldn't see much and they stood there, transfixed, staring into the inky black of the forest. The dogs were first to appear and then the lads saw the image that would be permanently etched upon their minds. It was a horse—a magnificent black stallion of fearsome size that exhaled plumes of fire, not air. Sitting astride this wondrous beast was the man the boys had heard about all their lives—Herne the Hunter, he of the antlered headdress and deerskin clothing. Face to face with what had until then only existed in their imaginations, the kids panicked and fled.

Herne the Hunter is among the more famous residents of Windsor Castle, a notable achievement considering his company. The castle, after all, has been used, off and on, as a

It's no surprise that England's Windsor Castle, a royal residence for centuries, is haunted by some famous spirits.

royal residence since William the Conqueror first chose the site to guard against a western invasion of London. Henry VIII, Elizabeth I, Charles I and George III all spent parts of their reigns in Berkshire. Queen Elizabeth II still uses Windsor as one of her main residences, making it the largest inhabited castle in the world. Even if Queen Elizabeth II chose not to live here, no one could say that the place is uninhabited. Windsor Castle is quite haunted, home to at least 25 ghosts, four of whom were once monarchs. Among the other 24 is Herne the Hunter, who has been seen on the castle grounds for several centuries.

No one knows for certain who Herne was in life. There is widespread belief that he served under Richard II as his chief gamekeeper and that the monarch owed his life to him. Just as an enraged stag was about to trample the king, Herne intervened, throwing himself between Richard II and the animal. He killed the stag, but he was mortally wounded in the process. Herne lay dying on the ground and only the intervention of a wizard saved him. Appearing before Herne, the wizard said that the hunter's life could be saved if the fallen stag's antlers were cut off and tied to Herne's head. It was done and Herne recovered to the great joy and relief of Richard II. Forever grateful to Herne, Richard II lavished praise and attention upon the hunter, much to the increasing displeasure of the other huntsmen. Already jealous of Herne's unparalleled prowess at hunting, the huntsmen were now incensed at this blatant favoritism. They devised a plan to rid themselves of Herne.

A rumor that Herne practiced witchcraft circulated quickly through Windsor Castle. It wasn't long before Richard II's subjects were calling for Herne's arrest. Witchcraft was heresy and its practitioners needed to be punished. Herne was scheduled to appear before the king but he never showed. Herne's body was found hanging from a tree in the Great Park just southeast of the castle. Not long after, the legend of Herne the Hunter was born.

Guards began reporting that while walking the Great Park and the Long Walk, they would hear the baying of hounds as well as a horn but would see nothing. Occasionally, witnesses

The White Drawing Room in Windsor Castle—possibly a favorite haunt of King Henry VIII.

saw Herne riding by, easily recognizable by the antlers on his head. Henry VIII himself claimed to have seen Herne the Hunter in 1509. In 1868, Queen Victoria was so disturbed by Herne's presence that she ordered the tree from which he had hanged himself cut down and used for firewood in the hopes of ridding Windsor Castle of his presence for good. England's longest-reigning monarch seemed to have good reason to exorcise Herne's spirit. His appearances over the years seem to be accompanied by national tragedy.

Herne is believed to have appeared on the eve of Henry IV's death in 1413 and just before Charles I's execution at the hands of Oliver Cromwell and the Parliamentarians in 1649. But despite Victoria's best efforts, Herne remained, visiting Windsor again in the days leading up to both world wars in 1914 and in 1939, before the Great Depression in 1931, preceding Edward VIII's abdication in 1936 and around the time of George VI's death in 1952. He has continued to appear at other times, although sightings are not necessarily a prelude to disaster. Herne has simply chosen to stay at Windsor Castle, along with a host of others.

Even before Herne's death, Windsor Castle had been the setting for the paranormal. In the 17th century, the ghost of the Duke of Buckingham appeared at Windsor Castle to pass a warning along to Captain Parker. Three times the Duke came, each time begging Parker to warn his son, Sir George Villiers, that unless he mended his ways, he would "live but for a short time." Parker did so, but the cavalier Villiers ignored the entreaties. Six months later, Villiers was dead, knifed to death by an assassin.

Queen Elizabeth I, a believer in spiritual phenomena, is said to have foreseen her own death in Windsor Castle. Just days after her death in 1603, terrified guards said that a woman dressed in black, with a black lace scarf draped across her head and shoulders, walked across the library only to disappear into the wall. The guards said that the woman was undoubtedly the resurrected spirit of their fallen queen.

Perhaps Elizabeth remains to keep her father, Henry VIII, company. He haunts the castle too. A gout sufferer forever

Arguably the most infamous monarch of all time, Henry VIII still haunts Windsor Castle.

hobbled by a hunting accident, Henry VIII announces his arrival with groans and the sound of his heavy, plodding footsteps. In 1977, two soldiers saw Henry VIII's ghost walking along a walkway and then vanish into a wall. Intrigued, the men managed to find faded and weathered plans for the castle. At the precise point where Henry VIII disappeared into the wall, there once stood a door. The door, in fact, was still there. It had only been bricked over. Renovations, apparently, meant little to the corpulent monarch. Clearly he likes things the way they were. So too does Charles I. Unlike some apparitions, who spend eternity looking for lost limbs, the king, beheaded by Oliver Cromwell, appears in the library, head intact, looking exactly as he does in Van Dyck's famous portrait. These monarchs, all related by blood, appear to their descendants still, reminding them that as representatives of the royal line, they must serve not only those alive today, but also those from years gone by.

Windsor Castle reveres the past. Buried underneath the Chapel of St. George are the bodies of Henry VIII, Charles I, George V and George VI. When fire gutted 100 rooms in 1992, five years and $59.2 million were spent painstakingly restoring the damaged rooms to their original Gothic glory. Seventy percent of the money came from the public, revealing Britons' adoration for a past that comes to life whenever someone sees Henry VIII, Elizabeth I or Herne the Hunter walking the grounds at Windsor Castle.

Mackenzie House
TORONTO, ONTARIO

While many believe that William Lyon Mackenzie only lived in the house at 82 Bond Street for a brief two years before his death in 1861, others feel that Mackenzie never really left the building. Toronto's first mayor still calls the place home, making the Mackenzie House the most haunted building of its kind in the city.

Born in Scotland, Mackenzie first came to Upper Canada in 1820. He saw inequities among class strata in Toronto that needed to be addressed. Too much political power was concentrated in too few hands and Mackenzie, influenced by American republicanism, was intent on change. He made his views clear in his paper, the *Colonial Advocate*, calling for an end to the Canadian oligarchy. Those in power felt sufficiently threatened to mob Mackenzie's printing press and hurl his equipment into the lake. Dressed as Indians, they had hoped to escape prosecution for their crime, but Mackenzie wasn't fooled. Neither were the courts. Mackenzie was awarded £625 in compensation (a rather hefty sum). The act only served to steel Mackenzie's resolve. Advocating change wasn't enough. A meeting with United States President Andrew Jackson convinced Mackenzie that he had to make it happen.

In 1828, he was elected to the House of Assembly for York County. His nomination indicated that his message resonated with a public weary of rulers who elevated themselves above the masses. But the ruling elite was not to be swayed. Deeming Mackenzie's scathing attacks in the *Colonial Advocate* as libelous, government officials decided that

A short man in a red wig and frock is often seen appearing and disappearing in Mackenzie House in Toronto, Ontario.

Mackenzie had abused his position and privilege. On those grounds, they expelled him from his seat only to see him reelected. Again, they dismissed him only to see him reelected once again. In total, Mackenzie was elected five times to a seat that the government was determined to refuse him. The aristocrats in the Family Compact refused to see that the more they attacked Mackenzie, the more emboldened he became.

The Family Compact consisted of a small group of public servants drawn from Canadian high society—individuals with strong ties to the British Empire. Based in York, they spurned the populist leanings of the United States and Mackenzie, choosing instead to align themselves with British institutions and manners. When York was incorporated as the city of Toronto in 1834, Mackenzie was desperate to keep the city from falling into the wrong hands. Rallying supporters through the *Colonial Advocate* and speeches, the Reformers overwhelmed the Tories in the elections. Mackenzie was chosen to be mayor. He only lasted one term, and in 1837 Mackenzie found himself without a post and the oligarchy back in power. He could not stand to see the English ignore locally elected legislators, viewing their intrusion as foreign imposition. Mackenzie felt rebellion was the only means of securing a true democracy.

Defeats at Montgomery's Tavern and Navy Island forced Mackenzie and his supporters to flee to the United States and begin cross-border raids upon Upper Canada. But the United States was less than willing to have its territory used as headquarters for an insurrection that might lead them into another conflict with the British Empire. The rebellion in Upper Canada came to an end when Mackenzie was arrested and sentenced to 18 months in prison for violating neutrality laws. Upon his release, Mackenzie found return to Canada impossible. Branded a traitor, Mackenzie was charged with high treason, a sentence punishable by death.

He spent 10 years in the United States, returning finally in 1849 when the government offered him a full pardon. His last years were spent dabbling occasionally in politics; Mackenzie's previous failures had jaded him, and he no longer approached his work with the enthusiasm and fervor of his youth. He retired from politics in 1859, a broken man. He was haunted by depression and hounded by creditors. His wife and friends pooled their resources to buy Mackenzie the gas-lit Victorian home at 82 Bond Street. Mackenzie passed away two years later in a second-floor bedroom.

Mackenzie House pays tribute to the first mayor of Toronto, a man who envisioned a government where everyone, regardless of status or wealth, has a voice. In death, Mackenzie seems to have rediscovered the zeal and enthusiasm missing from his twilight. Cold spots have been reported throughout the house, as well as phantom footsteps. In the basement, there is a printing press of the sort that Mackenzie himself might very well have used to print the *Colonial Advocate*. He's still at work, apparently; the printing press is known to jump into action free of human hands.

But Mackenzie's spirit is not all about work. Toilets that flush on their own and faucets that turn themselves on and off are also attributed to the playful ghost. Every now and then, he even makes an appearance, most often in the second-floor bedroom where he died. Visitors have seen a short man in a red wig and frock coat appear and disappear.

The activity was so pervasive at one point in the 1960s that Anglican Archdeacon John Frank held an exorcism. But it seems he still has some work to do. When the Toronto Historical Board took over the home, the members were given an official inventory. An entry among the list of items was "One Ghost (exorcised)." The many subsequent sightings and reports over the years would indicate that the official inventory should probably be revised.

Haw Branch Plantation
AMELIA COUNTY, VIRGINIA

Is it life that imitates art or art that imitates life? If the events that took place at the Haw Branch Plantation are any indication, life and art might very well be one and the same. In 1969, a cousin gave the McConnaughey family a portrait, reportedly rendered in brilliant pastel colors. It was of a distant relative named Florence Wright who died at 24 before her portrait was finished. Yet when the package was opened in the McConnaughey's sitting room at Haw Branch Plantation, the family's first question was whether or not their cousin was colorblind. They expected a portrait in brilliant color but discovered what looked to be a charcoal sketch. Still, they hung the large picture over the library fireplace and it sat there for months, undisturbed, until the day William Cary McConnaughey noticed the most peculiar thing. What followed was the culmination of psychic phenomena that began three months after the McConnaughey family moved into the historic home at Haw Branch in 1965.

Colonel Thomas Tabb and his wife first settled the land of Haw Branch in 1735. It wasn't long before Tabb was one of Virginia's largest landowners and most prosperous merchants. Drawing inspiration from the stands of hawthorn trees that lined a small stream running through his property,

Tabb christened his plantation Haw Branch. The property covered acres of verdant space and included impressive specimens of magnolia, elm and tulip.

By 1748, Tabb built a small home which his son, John Tabb, would later expand into the large Georgian–Federal-style mansion that became familiar throughout Amelia County for two centuries. After the Civil War, Haw Branch fell from prominence; all that remained of Tabb's former holdings were the house and a drastically diminished plantation. By the mid-20th century, the house had been abandoned. Its only residents were herds of cows that trampled through absent windows and empty doorways.

In 1965, Mary Gibson Jefferson, William McConnaughey's wife, was dismayed to learn what had happened at Haw Branch. As a child, her grandmother had taken her to visit the plantation, then already in ruins. Before its abandonment, Haw Branch had been the home to generations of Jeffersons since the plantation had been established in 1745. Mary's grandmother had lived there as a little girl and wanted to share a tangible part of the family's history with her granddaughter. Although only nine when she first saw the house, Mary could still remember the wistful look of longing in her grandmother's eyes as they explored the plantation's acres. She also recalled the pain that creased the elderly woman's brow when she saw how dilapidated the house had become. So when Mary's husband decided that a new home would be needed for their burgeoning family of six, she suggested buying and restoring her ancestral Amelia County home.

Renovations took three months with crews of more than 25 poring over every rotting inch of the mansion. The floor

Screams and shrieks disturb the sleep of occupants of Haw Branch Plantation in Amelia County, Virginia.

needed to be sanded 11 times and the crew lost track of how many times the exterior wood had to be painted. Mary Jefferson described to the Southwest Virginia Ghost Hunters Society how rotted and weathered the exterior was and how it "absorbed fresh paint like a sponge." The family and their two dogs, Porkchop and Blackie, moved into the home in August 1965. For a while, life was good.

But on November 23, the silence of the slumbering mansion was shattered when shrieks descended from the attic, waking the family from sleep. Terrified, the McConnaugheys gathered their four children and their two dogs, both of which were quivering in fear. An investigation of the attic in the morning revealed nothing unusual, so the family was at a loss to explain what had happened.

As the weeks passed and nothing else happened, the anxiety and trepidation faded away. Assuming that the earlier incident was an isolated one, the family began to believe that perhaps they had imagined the whole thing. Six months later, on May 23, 1966, the McConnaugheys were asleep when they were jarred from slumber by earsplitting shrieks. It happened again half a year later and then half a year after that. In the spring of 1968, the screams would be silenced.

Eager to trace the origin of the shrieks, the McConnaugheys set up a tape recorder on May 23, 1968. But that night, something quite different happened. They heard footsteps outside, accompanied by a mournful cry. The children said it was the call of a giant bird they had seen flying across the moonlit sky. The bird—if that was in fact what it was—was never seen again. But from that day on, something began to walk the halls of Haw Branch, a beautiful apparition of a woman in a flowing white skirt, first seen standing before the drawing room fireplace.

While getting a glass of milk one night, Mary had an unusual encounter that she described to the Southwest Virginia Ghost Hunters Society. She saw "the silhouette of a slim girl in a floor-length dress with a full skirt...she simply disappeared from one instant to the next." Her appearance seemed to herald the arrival of a host of other paranormal phenomena.

The McConnaugheys soon found themselves assaulted with phantom footsteps that echoed throughout the house.

Scrapes and squeaks came from the attic, as if furniture was being rearranged by some interior design-minded spirit. Of course, whenever the family inspected the room, it was undisturbed. Furniture still sat squat and solid underneath drop sheets. The dust collected on the floor was undisturbed and devoid of tracks. Peaceful evenings were interrupted constantly by loud thumps outside the windows, as if someone were dropping something heavy onto the ground. But when the family went outside to investigate, they found nothing but an empty lawn. Rooms filled with scents emanating from sources unknown. The Lady in White seemed particularly fond of oranges and roses; their aromas, in the absence of either, often announced her arrival.

Determined to learn more about the home, Mary set about asking family and close friends if anyone had ever experienced anything unusual when her ancestors lived in the house. Few remembered much about Haw Branch being haunted, but when Mary mentioned the Lady in White, her grandmother's face lit up with recognition.

As a child, the grandmother remembered how one morning her mother complained of a poor night's sleep because she had been awakened by a spirit dressed in shimmering white clothing. The ghost was apparently familiar with Mary's ancestors, for once when her great grandmother's name was mentioned, lights over the dining room table increased to a intensity of such brilliance that the family was forced to shield its eyes before the lights burned themselves out with a loud pop. Not long after, the family received the portrait of Florence Wright.

While passing through the library, McConnaughey would often feel as if he was interrupting a conversation. As he approached the room, he would hear snatches of conversation—as though women were huddled together whispering. Yet when he entered the library, the voices would stop and he found find himself utterly alone in the room. Then, while reading his newspaper one evening, McConnaughey happened to cast his gaze upon the portrait. He looked back down at his newspaper and then jerked his head back to look at the drawing. The newspaper fell from his hands and he walked over to the mantle, peering closely to get a better look. He rubbed his eyes, but he was not hallucinating. Somehow, the rose in Florence Wright's portrait was no longer gray, white or black. It was actually a light pink. And where her cheeks had once been devoid of color, Florence's face had acquired a flesh tone.

Over the next year, the colorization of the picture continued until the formerly black and white portrait was now a stunning palette of colors from all ends of the spectrum. Experts were brought in at various stages and each had no explanation to offer. They were only able to confirm that the portrait was somehow coloring itself. Psychic researchers brought into the home theorized that Florence Wright, who died as the portrait was being completed, was supernaturally tied to the portrait. Color drained out of it if she was unhappy, but with the help of the ethereal ladies whom William McConnaughey had heard chattering, she was able to register her happiness at being in Haw Branch.

Since the 1970s, many other spirits have appeared at Haw Branch, most of whose origins are unknown and histories long lost. One man roams the barn with a lit lantern. Approach him, and his form immediately dissolves into the night air, leaving behind the lantern to linger for a few moments more. Others include two other gentlemen in noticeable distress. One walks the grounds, dragging a lame leg behind him, while another, dressed impeccably in a three-piece suit and top hat, screams for help before vanishing. But its most famous resident is still that of Florence Wright, who still inhabits the portrait. It's believed that if one should stare long and hard enough at her, she will blush, uncomfortable with the attention her presence has aroused. In death, Wright became the very definition of living art.

The White House
WASHINGTON, D.C.

It is the very symbol of one of the world's most enduring republics—a gleaming monument in a city of white stone, statues, memorials and shrines celebrating the heroes and ideals of the country that began as a simple colony and rose to become one of the most powerful of nations. It is a grand building through which every president since John Adams has passed. With over 130 rooms, the simplicity of the building's name, the White House, belies the magnitude of its place in the American consciousness. The one constant during periods of revolution, secession and civil unrest has been the White House, a beacon to which the lost can turn to renew their frayed hopes and wavering faiths. How appropriate, then, that the ghost most commonly sighted in the White House is that of the president who guided the United States through its most divisive period, when the Civil War threatened to destroy the American republic.

The White House in Washington, D.C., remains home to ghosts of several former presidents and their family members.

Upon Abraham Lincoln's nomination as president of the United States in 1860, South Carolina immediately seceded from the Union. A host of others were quick to follow. By February 1861, the Confederate States of America had elected Jefferson Davis its president, and in April the opening shots of the Civil War were heard when Confederate troops opened fire on Fort Sumter. Lincoln, the unassuming man from the backwoods of Kentucky, was now charged with preserving the Union. "In your hands, my dissatisfied fellow countrymen," he said, "is the momentous issue of civil war. You have no oath registered in Heaven to destroy the government, while I shall have the most solemn one to preserve, protect and defend it." A pacifist, Lincoln would use force to bring the secessionists to their knees. He called upon 75,000 volunteers to form the Union Army. The war was now well and truly joined.

Lincoln monitored the war's progress from the room that now bears his name in the White House, the Lincoln Bedroom. During Lincoln's day, it was a personal office and Cabinet room, its walls festooned with maps upon maps of the Civil War. It was from here that Lincoln agonized over every Confederate victory, savored every Union triumph and cursed every soldier's death. And it was in this room that Lincoln transformed the war. Recognizing the northern public's growing demand for the abolition of slavery, Lincoln signed the Emancipation Proclamation in January 1863, freeing all the slaves in the Confederacy.

With the proclamation's passage, the war became not only a fight to preserve the Union, but also an attempt to end an institution that contradicted the very words on which the country had been founded, the self-evident truth that "all men are created equal." It was the precursor to the Thirteenth Amendment, the constitutional change that permanently abolished slavery. And while the act angered both radical Republicans, who thought Lincoln too cautious, and reactionary Republicans, who thought Lincoln too reckless, the fall of Atlanta at the hand of Sherman all but ensured that the president would remain in office for a second term.

Lincoln's first term was stressful; even in his private life he found no escape. He ministered constantly to his Southerner wife, Mary Todd, whose health faltered and wavered. Branded a traitor by the South and viewed with suspicion by the North, Mary sought solace in lavish entertainment and in the care of her husband. The death of their son Willie in 1862 from typhoid fever at the age of 12 only served to plunge Mary farther into the recesses of depression. Willie,

Willie Lincoln died young, but he has never really left the White House.

an intelligent child who bore many of his father's traits, took with him into death the dearest and greatest parts of his parents' souls.

"My poor boy," Lincoln said. "He was too good for this earth. God has called him home…I know he is much better off in heaven, but then we loved him so. It is hard, hard to have him die."

Willie lay in state in the Green Room next to the East Room in the White House before being buried in Oak Hill Cemetery. Upon Willie's death, Mary's well-known fascination with the Spiritualists and the occult began. Lincoln found himself watching his wife more closely than ever, worried that her naïveté would make her easy prey for charlatans. She had no head for finance, blithely contacting self-proclaimed psychics and mediums for séances in the White House. Whether she ever managed to contact her dear son Willie is up for debate, but Lincoln did tolerate these flights of fancy, acknowledging the pacifying effect they had on his wife. In time, she regained enough of herself to throw herself fully into her husband's campaign for a second term as president.

With the Confederacy teetering on the brink of surrender, strong Northern morale carried Lincoln into the White House for a second time in November 1864. The Union was very nearly secure and the abolition of slavery was all but final—political successes that gave Lincoln a brief respite from the agonies of war. Sadly, he was unable to enjoy the spoils of victory for long.

The man who had dedicated his presidency to preserving the Union and to easing reconstruction was assassinated in Ford's Theater on April 14, 1865, while watching a play. His assailant was actor John Wilkes Booth, a Southern sympathizer who believed Lincoln's death would reverse the course of war. Surgeons worked throughout the night to save the fallen president, but as the sun rose in the east, Lincoln had already faded into the west. At 7:20 on the morning of April 15, 1865, Abraham Lincoln was pronounced dead.

His body lay in state in the East Room and then was placed aboard a train, to be taken back to Springfield, Illinois, his adopted home. At every one of its stops, from Philadelphia to New York to Columbus to Indianapolis, tens and sometimes hundreds of thousands would line up to catch a brief glimpse. Three hundred mourners accompanied Lincoln on his trip; alongside him in the funeral car was the coffin of Willie Lincoln. Father and son had been reunited.

Not long after Lincoln's death, people began hearing rumors that Lincoln had foreseen his own death—and so had Mary Todd. Just days before the assassination, Lincoln awoke from slumber, terrified by things that had happened in his dream. He described the dream to a friend, Ward Hill Lamon. Lamon later retold Lincoln's account in his book, *Recollections of Abraham Lincoln.* Lincoln dreamed of being drawn down the White House halls by the sounds of "subdued sobs, as if a number of people were weeping." He was "determined to find the cause of a state of things so mysterious and so shocking."

Lincoln explained to Lamon: "I kept on until I arrived at the East Room, which I entered. There I met with a sickening surprise. Before me was a corpse in funeral vestments. Around it were stationed soldiers who were acting as guards, and there was a throng of people, some gazing mournfully upon the corpse, whose face was covered, others weeping pitifully. 'Who is dead in the White House?' I demanded of one of the soldiers. 'The President,' was his answer. 'He was killed by an assassin!' I slept no more that night, and although it was only a dream, I have been strangely annoyed by it ever since."

Lincoln wasn't alone in his foreboding. One evening, while looking in a mirror, he saw not one but two reflections of his face. One was pale and the other disappeared when he cast his gaze upon it. When Mary Todd witnessed the phenomenon, she warned her husband that while he would win another term in the White House, he would not live to see its conclusion.

Although she had been forewarned of her husband's impending doom, Mary Todd was devastated upon his assassination. She spent the next 17 years of her life wandering Europe and America, tormented by accusations that she had stolen materials from the White House and that she had gone insane. When son Tad died in 1871, his older brother Robert had Mary Todd committed to an asylum. Mary was granted her freedom only a year later, but the damage had been done. She would never forgive her eldest son for such a betrayal. Her health deteriorated rapidly. She died in 1882 at her sister's home in Springfield, Illinois, in the very bedroom in which she and Abraham had spent their wedding night so many years before. On her finger was the ring Lincoln had inscribed with the words "Love is Eternal." So too, it seems, is her husband.

Some question whether Abraham Lincoln has ever truly left the White House. Jacqueline Kennedy, the wife of another assassinated president, reportedly felt Lincoln's presence in the house and took great comfort in it. Indeed, Lincoln is said to have appeared to John F. Kennedy to warn him not to travel to Dallas in November 1963. He did, and Camelot was soon without its king. President Truman was sound asleep one night when three loud knocks on his door roused him from slumber. Yet when he answered the door, there was nobody there. When he later spoke about the incident, he said, "Damned place is haunted, sure as shootin.'"

Not surprisingly, Lincoln is said to have appeared most frequently during President Franklin D. Roosevelt's terms in the White House. Both men, after all, led the country through tumultuous times. Lincoln had the Civil War; Roosevelt had the Great Depression and World War II. During the 13 years that Eleanor used the Lincoln Bedroom as her study, she consistently felt the Great Emancipator's presence in the room. One of Roosevelt's valets caught a glimpse of Lincoln's ghost and promptly fled the house, claiming he would never return. One of Eleanor's maids remained much calmer when she saw Lincoln sitting on a bed, pulling off a pair of boots. His arrival was always precipitated by the barking of the Roosevelts' Scottish terrier Fala.

Others maintained that Lincoln could still be seen in the Lincoln Bedroom, staring out the window, pondering the fate of the nation. Carl Sandburg, Lincoln's biographer, felt Lincoln stand beside him. Sir Winston Churchill refused to stay in the Lincoln Bedroom after seeing the dead president's apparition. And Queen Wilhemina of the Netherlands almost died of fright when she answered a knock at her door during a stay at the White House. When she opened the door, she saw the ghost of Lincoln standing before her.

But Lincoln is not alone. There are other spirits maintaining residence in the White House. During President Ulysses S. Grant's administration, members of Grant's staff and family sensed the presence of a child in a number of the house's second-floor bedrooms. The Grants even reported having conversations with the child. President Lyndon B. Johnson's daughter, Lynda Johnson Robb, felt the same presence. The consensus is that the calming presence they felt had to be that of Willie Lincoln.

Sightings of the two Lincoln ghosts dropped off after President Harry Truman renovated the White House. During his administration, the mansion was near collapse. Rather than tear it down and rebuild, its exterior walls were shored up while the interior was taken apart and reassembled with as much of the original material as possible. The project took four years to complete, during which time Truman also added a balcony on the south portico. The changes were far from drastic, but the construction was apparently a significant disruption. Since then, sightings of Lincoln's ghost have become altogether rare. Maureen Reagan apparently saw the ghost, and the Reagans' dog Rex refused to enter the Lincoln Bedroom. Heavy footfalls echoed through empty hallways every now and then, while phantom knocks on doors would rouse sleepers from slumber.

The Clintons never reported any encounters with the paranormal, but Hillary Rodham Clinton always felt that there was something unusual in the atmosphere. "Something about the house at night," she once said on the *Rosie O'Donnell Show*, "you just feel like you are summoning up the spirits of all the people who have lived there and walked through the halls." President Clinton's press secretary, Mike McCarry, was a little more blunt. "Serious people," he said to CNN in 1997, "have some serious tales to tell." Many members of Clinton's staff refused to enter the Lincoln Bedroom for the same reasons that Sir Winston Churchill had. Lincoln had yet to leave.

Whaley House
SAN DIEGO, CALIFORNIA

Long before Kathie Lee Gifford and *Who Wants to Be a Millionaire*, Regis Philbin and a friend decided to spend a night in Whaley House. Ever since it opened its doors as a museum in 1960, Whaley House had been the subject of much speculation and rumor. To put it more accurately, it wasn't so much the house as what went on inside that sparked the collective curiosity of San Diego. There were rumors that the place was haunted and that its builder and his immediate family, the last of whom passed away in 1953, still resided at the house.

In 1964, Philbin was the host of a local television show. He set out to prove the existence or non-existence of the Whaley ghosts. Whaley House was empty when he and his friend arrived. At 2:30 in the morning, Philbin saw something. He saw someone walk from the study to the music room. Grabbing a flashlight, Philbin shone it upon the figure to get a better look. But when the beam of light struck the figure, it vanished. Philbin and his friend were thoroughly frightened. They fled.

When people heard about Philbin's experience, Whaley House's reputation as a haunted house was cemented. Visitors who came to experience the paranormal included *Twilight Zone* creator Rod Serling and celebrated horror film actor Vincent Price. The stories were so persistent that within a few short years the United States Commerce Department officially recognized Whaley House as being haunted—one of only 29 homes in the country to receive such recognition. Some researchers consider Whaley House the most haunted house in America. If accounts are accurate, then there is no shortage of spirits inside. There are ghosts hailing from the 19th century, as well as apparitions of man, woman and child. Some have been identified, while others remain an enigma.

Two scents frequently waft through the halls of Whaley House. One is the smell of tobacco; the other is that of flowery perfume. The locals take the former as a sign that Thomas Whaley is near, while the latter marks the presence of his wife Anna. Thomas, who died in 1890, has never left the home he built.

The smell of tobacco is sometimes accompanied by Thomas' boisterous laugh. And while his spirit, clad in frock coat and top hat, has been seen throughout the home, he is most often seen at the top of the stairs or in the master bedroom, letting all know that he is still master of the house. His wife still plays the host. Her love of music continues after death in the form of impromptu concerts in the house. People are known to pause during tours of the house when their ears are treated to the beautiful and haunting melodies that come from Anna's voice and piano.

Thomas Whaley left New York for San Diego by 1848. He settled in a neighborhood of 250 people known as Old Town and opened a store that catered to both colonial and aboriginal customers. The business proved profitable, and its success was mirrored in Thomas' family life with the birth of his son Francis. With plans for a large family, Thomas purchased several acres of land and began construction on a two-story, Greek Revival-style brick house. Construction of the home wasn't necessarily the beginning of the end for Thomas

A number of criminal executions on the Whaley House property have resulted in some dramatic hauntings.

Whaley, but life was far from ideal. From the start, the Whaleys were forced to share their home.

Thomas' land once served as the public hanging grounds of San Diego. Many convicts and criminals were executed on Whaley's property. As is well known, dramatic deaths are often a prelude to a haunting. Thomas' house proved to be no exception. Within months of moving in, he wrote to family members about hearing phantom footsteps upstairs and attributed their presence to the spirit of one James "Yankee Jim" Robinson.

Yankee Jim had stolen a pilot boat in 1852. A concerned citizen recognized the thief while walking through Old Town. Instead of summoning the authorities, the citizen took action, butting Yankee Jim in the head with the hilt of his sword. Yankee Jim was wounded and he collapsed to the ground. His trial was a farce. Suffering from a serious wound, Yankee Jim was in no way fit to stand trial. Denied medical treatment, the wound turned noxious, causing Yankee Jim to arrive at his trial barely conscious. He was convicted of theft and sentenced to death by public hanging. The only problem, though, was Yankee Jim's height.

Yankee Jim was taller than the average person. The public gallows had not been designed for someone of his height. When mules pulled the wagon from under his feet, his neck didn't snap as intended. His feet grazed the ground, and while it wasn't enough to save his life, it was just enough to delay the inevitable. Yankee Jim twisted and turned from the gallows, requiring almost an hour to die.

Coincidentally, whenever Thomas stood in the archway between his parlor and music room, he would feel strangled. The archway stood where the public gallows had once been. In the 1960s, a psychic named Kay Sterner visited Whaley House. As she walked under the archway, she had a vision of mules pulling a wagon out from under scaffolding. Sterner had no previous knowledge of the house's history.

Yankee Jim's death is but one small chapter in the home's long story. Tragedy struck the Whaleys when their firstborn son, Francis Hinton, died at 17 months of scarlet fever. Francis was a Whaley, though, and in keeping with the family

A bedroom in Whaley House, which now serves as a museum.

tradition, the baby continues to haunt the room in which he died. His cries can be heard echoing throughout the house. The family pet, Dolly, still runs through the halls too. The small dog wanders from room to room, only to vanish moments later.

In the kitchen, hanging utensils stir when air is still, as if caressed by a breeze. The mischief is often accompanied by girlish laughter—attributed to the little red-haired girl dressed in late 19th-century clothing. The little child is believed to be the ghost of one the Whaley children's playmates. When the girl ran into a low-hanging clothesline, the impact crushed her trachea and she died while being carried into the kitchen. She developed a postmortem fondness for items in the kitchen—notably a teapot and a meat cleaver—but lost none of her youthful playfulness.

The last of the Whaleys to live in the house was Corinne, who died in 1953. While there were plans to demolish the brick house, Old Town fought to preserve the home. Today it serves as a museum. The Whaleys must be thrilled, even if they are not fond of large crowds. It's said that one evening, after a particularly busy day at the museum, each door and window was slammed shut simultaneously. Accustomed to the Whaleys and their habits, exhausted museum staff could only share in the ghosts' collective relief.

The Spy House
PORT MONMOUTH, NEW JERSEY

Those in charge of the museum deny that ghosts ever roamed the halls of what is believed to be the oldest house in New Jersey. But there was a time when the Spy House Museum in Port Monmouth was embraced for its past—a past that refused to die and revealed itself through at least two dozen spirits.

They included 24 ghosts spanning three centuries and ranging from Native Americans and American patriots to lovelorn wives and swarthy pirates. Not surprisingly, thousands flocked to Port Monmouth to take in ghost tours run by museum founder Gertrude Neidlinger and led by psychic Jane Doherty—at least until Neidlinger was forced to cede control of her work to the board of trustees in the early 1990s. The tours stopped, the furniture was changed and dirt was brought in to fill a cellar that had been one of the most highly anticipated stops in the ghost tour.

Museum staff insisted that Neidlinger wasn't entirely sane, that the Spy House's haunting had been cooked up to garner interest and publicity. It did and also attracted people interested in the fantastic. Regardless, there are those who still believe in the Spy House's haunting—those who acknowledge that the Spy House was once known as one of the top three haunted places in the United States, and those who know that concerted denials are not enough to exorcise the ghosts of the past.

The Spy House was not always known as such. The oldest parts of the venerated building began as a one-room cabin that Thomas Whitlock built in 1648. As the 18th century approached, the home was enlarged through the addition of three other buildings. In 1696, Daniel Seabrook, who had married into Whitlock's family, bought the house. Almost a century later, the colonials had had enough of what they perceived to be British exploitation of their labor and their freedoms. The shots fired at Lexington and Concord in 1775 signaled the beginning of the American Revolution, a war that was fully joined with the signing of the Declaration of Independence in 1776.

Those living in Daniel Seabrook's old house believed in the creation of a country they could call their own—a free land where they could live independent of colonial rule. To help the cause, the house was transformed into an inn that catered to British soldiers. But before the soldiers could lay their weary heads down for the night, they were plied with alcohol in the inn's tavern. Inebriation loosened the lips; drunken British soldiers caroused well into the night and, listening to their raucous conversations in rooms upstairs through the floor, were colonial spies. From their perches, these spies were able to learn which British ships had been left unmanned in the harbors of Sandy Hook Bay. Under cover of darkness, with the drunken revelries of British soldiers as their accompaniment, the spies would steal into the harbor to sabotage the unattended ships.

British officers soon suspected that the recent misfortunes their navy had suffered in the harbor had its origins in the inn they frequented so often. The name "Spy House" was uttered not long after with distaste. The British attempted to strike at the root of their problems by setting fire to the Spy House, but watchful women thwarted their efforts by extinguishing the fire with water from their washing buckets. But even when the United States of America had achieved its complete independence through the Treaty of Paris, a British presence remained in the Spy House.

Long after he left America for Britain as the man who surrendered to the colonials, Lord Charles Cornwallis continued to frequent the tavern he had enjoyed so much when stationed in New Jersey. Previous residents of the Spy House often encountered the general's spirit in the halls. Usually Cornwallis was quite drunk. He subjected the living to long-winded rants about his halcyon days as a brilliant war strategist while staggering about the house, lurching into walls and doors. But his tirades are not the only sounds to echo throughout the house.

In 1800, a pirate named Captain Morgan took over the Spy House, using it to imprison a wealthy French family he had captured while at sea. For three months Morgan waited for the arrival of the family's ransom, during which time he and his crew beat the captive men mercilessly and assaulted the women. There is some question as to whether or not Morgan was ever paid his ransom. After all, the French family was killed, the women strangled, the men beaten. Morgan, though, met the same fate at nature's hands when a squall sank his ship in the Caribbean.

Instead of descending to Hell, Morgan returned to the Spy House to torment and taunt its residents with a stream of invective and curses that could only come from an evil soul. But perhaps he has returned for another reason altogether. Accompanying the captain is his first mate, a man who seeks absolution for a life lived in sin. He begs forgiveness from those who see him, offering a hidden treasure trove in the house's cellar as a tithe. Morgan wants to drive the living away, lest they get their greedy hands on his hard-earned wealth.

Not all the spirits of the Spy House are so ill-mannered. There are forlorn ghosts here too—spirits who roam the house weighed down with remorse for lives lived in pain and suffering. There is Penelope, a woman whom God blessed with the desire to be a mother, but left her unable to carry a child. Upon her death, she remained at the Spy House, appearing to mothers with young children, sometimes reaching out as if to hold the child.

Abigail, the woman in black, paces in front of the window with her eyes fixed on the horizon, watching for the ship bearing her husband to return. But the ship will never arrive because her husband, a sea captain, died at sea long ago. Lydia Longstreet Seabrook, the so-called woman in white, walks the staircase of the Spy House and rests in the Blue and White Rooms of the home. In those rooms, she leans over nothing and adjusts something with her hands that only she can see. To those who have seen Lydia, her actions suggest that she sees a crib before her and is tending to a child within.

Drivers passing the house are shocked when a girl appears before them too suddenly and quickly for them to stop their cars. They pass through the girl, horrified at the idea that they might have just killed a young child. But when they get out to check on the body, the girl is alive and well. Or so one might believe. She is a ghost, of course, a child killed so many years ago when a horse and wagon ran her down. In eternity, she is condemned for whatever reason to relive the last precious moments of her life, much like the other children who haunt the Spy House.

A young spirit known only as Walter makes his home in the attic, descending at times to search for his long-lost dead mother. Peter, an 11-year-old who died in the 1700s, wants nothing more than to be a part of a family. He has a habit of becoming an overnight guest at the homes of museum visitors. Psychic Jane Doherty recalled how a skeptical man laughingly invited Tom to come home with him and his wife. The next day, she received a phone call from the man, who was desperate to know how to rid his home of the spirit. When the man and his wife had settled down to sleep the evening before, they both noticed that the room was getting cold. The man turned the thermostat, which was already at 70, even higher. Yet still they shivered. They brought out extra blankets to keep themselves warm, all under the watchful stare of a hazy apparition standing next to their bed.

There is every reason to believe that the Spy House has been haunted ever since its first resident, Thomas Whitlock, died. His apparition has been seen in the front hall of the home, puffing on a pipe. When Whitlock lived in the home, he contended with the threat of attack from Native American tribes, irate that their lands had been confiscated. Whitlock kept a constant vigil, wary of Indians who might be peering into his house through its windows. It's said that these Indians still do, but that Whitlock has learned to live peacefully with his former enemies. Instead, he passes his afterlife smoking his pipe, walking through his home and flirting with the women who walk its halls. He is fond of pinching women and pulling on their hair.

With such a rich collection of phantoms, the Spy House's ghost tours, begun in 1990, seemed a natural step in the museum's evolution. It was the brainchild of the woman who had saved New Jersey's oldest house. Gertrude Neidlinger had retired from a life as a concert singer and decided that she would spend the rest of her life dedicated to preserving and celebrating the history of Port Monmouth. She and her brother acquired the house in the 1960s to use as a living museum of sorts. With over 30 years in the home, Neidlinger experienced too many things she was unable to explain away. She became convinced that the home was haunted and wanted a way to let people experience and see something of the afterlife for themselves. Financially strapped, the museum also needed the money that would be generated from the tours.

The tours' popularity soon eclipsed the museum itself. Paranormal enthusiasts, as well as curious amateurs, swarmed Port Monmouth, eager to catch a glimpse of the world's mysterious underbelly. News crews attempting to film the home found freshly charged batteries suddenly drained of all power. Recordings and photographs made in the cellar, where Captain Morgan's treasure is reportedly buried, never came out clearly. Dread and terror overtook visitors in the cellar—not surprising, perhaps, given the cellar's past as a slaughterhouse, prison, torture room and hideout. Word of mouth and media reports spread the Spy House's fame across the nation.

It was then that the museum's board of trustees ousted Neidlinger. As a museum staffer told writer Randolph Liebeck, who wrote about the home for *Weird NJ* magazine in October 1997, Neidlinger was "just crazy…she was driving this place down with that nonsense." The cellar was filled with dirt and reports of hauntings were denied. Tours are no longer given and because of funding cuts the museum is only open on weekends. What skeptics failed to realize was that in the Spy

House, the ghosts are a very real and tangible part of its history. They are living embodiments of all that the Spy House was and is. Long after their deaths, the resident spirits breathe life into the Spy House's past, haunted or not.

Woodburn Mansion
DOVER, DELAWARE

Lorenzo Dow awoke in his guest bed, renewed after a long day of traveling. It didn't hurt that he had rested in the Middle Georgian splendor of a home owned by his friends, Dr. Martin Bates and his wife Mary. Dow, a Methodist preacher unaccustomed to the sort of opulence the home offered, marveled at the hand-carved woodworking and the Bates' fine collection of furniture and delicate china. He said as much to the man he passed on the staircase on his way to breakfast with the Bates. The man said nothing and continued quietly up the steps. Dow didn't think anything of the man's silence; it was early, after all, and perhaps he would loosen up after a bowl of oatmeal and a couple cups of coffee had warmed his blood.

Dow walked into the kitchen to find the Bates already there. They told him to sit down, so he did. Dow couldn't help noticing that the table had only been set for three. He said nothing about it, but when he noticed the Bates staring at him expectantly, he asked them what they wanted. They answered that they were waiting for him to say grace. Dow replied that he couldn't, that he'd prefer to wait for their other guest to arrive before he did so. The Bates looked at him quizzically. Dow was their only guest. Dow of course claimed that he'd said hello and good morning to a man on the steps not more than ten minutes earlier, a man in powdered wig, knee britches and a ruffled shirt. Dr. Bates' face darkened with each passing word, and when Dow was finished he looked positively frightened.

Dow had just provided the Bates with a perfect description of Bates' long-dead father. All seated around the breakfast table that morning in 1824 realized that Dow had encountered a ghost, the vaporous form of Dr. Bates' father risen from the dead. Woodburn Mansion was less than 40 years old and it had already experienced its first haunting. The Bates lived for eight years at Woodburn, accompanied by Dr. Bates' dead father. On different occasions, a number of guests fainted when the specter of the elderly Bates would materialize on an armchair in front of the fire.

Charles Hillyard built the Bates' home in 1790. It was one of the grandest ever in Delaware, situated among stands of old pines and poplars. In fact, the house is such a marvel that its residents have been reluctant to leave, even after they have become food for worms.

Although Bates' father was the first apparition sighted within Woodburn's halls, he has apparently found a different place to haunt. Today, the most commonly discussed phenomenon is the continuing presence of Woodburn's creator and original inhabitant, Charles Hillyard. Hillyard preferred to end his days flush with the warmth of inebriation. He would sit in his leather armchair, gazing out his window towards the woods beyond with a snifter of brandy in hand. In the cold Delaware winters, Hillyard enjoyed watching the snow fall as the liquor warmed his heart. Death has not kept him from his most cherished habit.

Woodburn Mansion in Dover, Delaware, continues to be haunted by its creator and first inhabitants.

Woodburn residents have often awakened in the morning to find decanters, freshly filled with wine the night before, empty. Sometimes half-full glasses of liquor left over from dinner parties were found drained the following day. Delaware Governor Charles Terry, Jr., who served from 1965 until 1969 and was the first Delaware governor to use Woodburn Mansion as an official residence, complained that the ghost of Charles Hillyard was siphoning off wine from vintage bottles he kept in the mansion's cellar. One of Terry's attendants rubbed his eyes and then rubbed them again when he walked into the kitchen one evening and saw the apparition of a man pour himself a drink from a decanter in the living room.

Jeanne Tribbit, wife of Governor Sherman W. Tribbit, is said to have actively baited the thirsty spirit, regularly leaving out bottles and glasses of wine for him during her years in the house from 1973 to 1977. No one knows why, but apparently she met with little success. Some students were subsequently invited to the home to conduct séances and use Ouija boards. Their efforts turned up nothing either. It seemed as if Hillyard could not be coaxed into coming out to play. Some skeptics began to question whether Woodburn was ever truly haunted. But if Hillyard had in fact finally abandoned his house, there is little doubt that there were other spirits eager to take up his torch.

In 1985, at an inauguration party held for incoming Governor Michael Castle, numerous guests in attendance kept complaining about someone who was tugging on their clothing. Yet when they looked down to see who was trying to draw their attention, there was no one there. But then it happened. A woman, drink in hand, peered into the corner of the house and caught a glimpse of a little girl dressed in a red gingham dress. The child looked forlorn and lonely, the combination arousing maternal instincts in the woman. She walked over to the corner to see if she could help the child but stopped dead when the girl just disappeared. Although she knew that she hadn't had too much to drink, she attributed the girl's appearance to slight inebriation.

But soon enough the woman learned that she wasn't the only one who saw the little girl. It soon came to light that the little girl, whose origins remain a mystery, had first started appearing to Woodburn guests and residents in the 1940s, often playing by the pool in the garden. Governor Castle continued to encounter her ghost and even permitted a teacher and three of her students to spend the night in the house. While nothing terribly unusual happened, the children were thoroughly convinced of the house's paranormal energy by morning. They claimed a restless night of sleep, caused by a portrait of a woman in one of the rooms. According to the children, she knowingly smiled at them throughout the night. They should be thankful that they didn't encounter one of the more malevolent spirits of Woodburn.

When Daniel Cowgill bought Woodburn from the Bates family, the Civil War was imminent. A Quaker, Cowgill had become convinced that slavery was a wrong that had to be righted. He freed his slaves, and when he first heard word about the Underground Railroad—used by fugitive slaves on their journey to freedom—he offered use of his home as a stop. Slaves hid in his cellar and then, through a tunnel that had been carved out of the earth, they would make their way to the St. Jones River where boats were waiting to ferry them across the Delaware River to the slave-free state of New Jersey. It was dangerous and deadly work. Slave owners didn't take kindly to being robbed of their property and often sent out raiders to bring the slaves back.

One evening, a band of raiders arrived at Woodburn, demanding that Cowgill send out the slaves. Cowgill refused and drove off the intruders, save for one who managed to stay behind. He had crawled up into a large poplar tree in the yard and remained immune to detection through the thick foliage. It's not known what his plan was,

A Canada goose mysteriously larks about the stairway at Woodburn, the scene of several paranormal events.

but it's clear he didn't succeed. The raider was trying to work his way down from the tree when he slipped and his head became lodged between two branches. He tried screaming for help but he couldn't even draw a breath. His legs flailed and he pushed with all his strength against the tree's branches as they squeezed the life out of him, hoping that he might jar himself loose. By the next morning, he was dead.

Until the tree was cut down in 1998, the raider was believed to have relived his agonizing death every Halloween. According to reports, those who walked by the tree late at night could see his hapless figure struggling to get free. Those in the house could hear the sounds of rattling chains. The tree was subsequently cut down. Ever since, Woodburn has been free of the Southern raider who died so long ago.

6
Colonial
Estates

North America's early history is rich with tales of espionage, war and changing fortunes. As revolutionaries struggled to free the colonies from the British, many remnants of the old world order resisted, especially in the South where traditionalists were reluctant to abandon their European ways. It's no coincidence that such a historically pivotal period has left behind its share of fascinating ghost stories. Rich in detail, these accounts reflect an emerging nation's struggle to define itself.

Oak Alley Plantation
VACHERIE, LOUISIANA

After an unknown Frenchman arrived in Louisiana long ago, he built himself a small house as shelter from the hot and humid conditions of the Mississippi delta. He also planted, in two evenly spaced rows, 28 oak trees, 14 in each row, 80 feet apart. Long after the Frenchman had passed on and his house had collapsed, the trees still stood. Once saplings, the oak trees now loom large over the landscape, casting rippling shadows where once sunlight baked the earth. And in place of a ramshackle hut sagging against the ground stands a grand plantation house.

The mansion is impressive in the way that homes of southern antebellum plantations should be. Twenty-eight columns support the structure, each a full 8 feet in circumference. Ceilings are 15 feet high, while the elements are kept at bay by brick walls 16 inches thick. The mansion is framed by a verandah, where many a homeowner has sat in the Louisiana afternoon heat to enjoy the vistas and an occasional mint julep. The home is named for the oak trees that line the path to the Mississippi River. With such a bucolic setting, those who have come to its grounds have had difficulty leaving it. Some residents, in fact, have never left Oak Alley, not even after the passage of two centuries. It's not known for certain who exactly haunts the estate today, but some theorize that the ghost could be the spirit of one of two women, either a mother or her daughter.

In the 1730s, Jacques Roman arrived in Louisiana from Grenoble, France, to help his cousin manage his affairs.

The lane of picturesque oak trees that gave Oak Alley Plantation in Vacherie, Louisiana, its name

Having been granted a large tract of land just west of New Orleans, the cousin, nobleman Joseph Paris du Vernay, required an extra set of hands to shoulder his new responsibilities. In 1741, Vernay married a Canadian named Marie D'Aigle and proceeded to amass a fortune through the acquisition and disposition of plantation property. Three of five children lived to inherit the fortune and property their father had acquired throughout the years.

With their wealth, these Creoles (or children of European parents) rose quickly through the ranks of the socially prominent in Louisiana. Son Andre was twice governor of Louisiana. Plantations of sugar prospered in St. James Parish. Cattle herds flourished in St. Landry Parish, while the family thrived in grand homes scattered throughout New Orleans. One of the children was Jacques Etienne Vernay, whose youngest son Jacques Telesphore Vernay would acquire the property known as Oak Alley and set in motion a chain of events that would lead to Oak Alley's haunting.

Jacques Telesphore Vernay fell in love with Celina Pilie, who came from a family with enough status and prominence to rival the Vernays. Celina's brother, Valcour, saw in the potential union an opportunity to further not only his family's social standing, but also his business. He owed a sizeable amount of money to a bank, so in exchange for the some help and land, he would give the Oak Alley Plantation to Jacques Telesphore Vernay. In June 1834, Jacques Telephore and Celina were married. By 1839, the plantation house was completed and while Celina named her home Bon Sejour, the name never took. Oak Alley it was and Oak Alley it would stay. And so too would one of the family members.

Louise Roman was Jacques and Celina's daughter. They had brought her up to believe in the tenets of the Catholic Church and to value her Creole heritage. So when she entered her twenties and suitors began to court her hand in marriage, she found that few could measure up to the standards she expected of a potential husband. Her disapproval carried with it the weight of her family name; most of those whom she rejected accepted their denial.

But for one, dogged determination was to be his reinforcement and he persisted in his pursuit, refusing to yield. The more she retreated, the more aggressive he became, until finally he attempted to take by force what was then a husband's right in the shadow of the oak trees. He threw himself at her, determined to force her to love him. Louise, however, proved as wily physically as she was emotionally. She kneed her attacker in the groin and while he lay on the ground, doubled over and writhing in pain, she ran.

She did not escape without incident, though. Dresses at the time were ill-suited for running. Yards of heavy material and the heavy iron hoop frame upon which the dress' skirt hung caused Louise to trip and cut her leg on the iron frame. In the days before inoculations against tetanus and other infections, Louise's wound festered. Gangrene set in. Doctors were forced to amputate her leg lest she die from the gangrene.

Louise survived. The leg did too. Her parents didn't want their daughter greeting her maker incomplete, so the leg was preserved to accompany Louise into the afterlife. But while the leg was preserved in a room in Oak Alley, something of the incident that almost took Louise's life survived. When her blood touched the earth, something of her spirit seeped into the ground and took root. For while Louise lived the rest of her life quietly in a convent in New Orleans, without the gruesome tragedies that are often the precursor to a haunting, her spirit has been seen running through Oak Alley.

Visitors and tourists have been startled when they see the transparent figure of a woman with long dark hair race by. The wind carries her 19th-century dress behind her. Louise rushes into the shadows of the oak trees where she disappears, leaving many a puzzled witness to wonder whether he or she really saw a ghost or just dreamed it.

But Louise's racing form is not the only apparition to surprise unwitting visitors. People touring the plantation house are often treated to a show as lights go off and on under their own power. Unseen hands touch visitors on the arm, while they find their olfactory senses overcome by the smell of lavender. A phantom carriage, no less, is known to rattle along the gravel path to the front door, bearing unseen passengers. And up along the widow's walk that overlooks the Mississippi River   where Celine used to stand watch for Jacques' return from business—Celine's spirit remains. Clad in black, she wanders the area, unable to leave the home that she loved so much. Tourists have been known to take photographs of empty rooms in Oak Alley and later notice a young woman with long dark hair staring out a window in their pictures.

Even time is affected in the halls of Oak Alley. According to a tradition of the antebellum South, when a house's owner dies, the clocks are stopped at the time of death. When, in 1972, the house passed into the hands of the Oak Alley Foundation, an organization dedicated to the preservation of the house, all clocks had been set to 7:30. Over the years, no one has touched the clocks again, yet somehow each clock now shows a different time. Perhaps some ornery spirits are unhappy that the clocks should only mark the passing of the home's most recent owner and not the rest. After all, a succession of owners came and went after the Romans' passing, each with their own particular stories and histories. Other paranormal events here hint at a dark side of the house's history.

One woman walking through the house on a tour was suddenly inundated by images of a struggle. She saw two men fighting to beat back a Confederate soldier. They threw the soldier onto his back with a snap. The soldier shrieked in agony, clutching at his back in pain. They beat his head against the verandah until he lay senseless, bloodied and battered. The soldier's body was dragged to the river and unceremoniously dumped into the Mississippi. Another visitor walking the verandah suddenly experienced sharp stabbing pains in his back—sensations that only subsided when moved away from the spot. A guide told him that he'd been standing in the spot where the alleged struggle between two men and a Confederate soldier had taken place so many years ago.

Oak Alley is open to visitors all year and is now both a plantation and a bed and breakfast. But for those who have witnessed something beyond explanation, Oak Alley will forever remain a haunted remnant of days long past.

Bishop Huntington House
HADLEY, MASSACHUSETTS

Things have changed little in Hadley since English settlers first founded the settlement in 1659 and hoped to earn their living from the land. To be sure, Hadley is not a relic of the past, but at its heart it remains a place whose fortunes are tethered to the whimsy of nature. The community has weathered drought, disease and soil depletion, but has never lost faith in what it once was and what it could be again. It has been built, torn down and rebuilt again in the same image over the centuries. Time is as much a commodity here as the corn, potatoes and tobacco—crops that form the backbone of Hadley's economy.

Nowhere is the past better embodied than in Bishop Huntington House, a former house turned historical museum. To step through the house's doors is to reach back 250 years, to a time before America was even a nation. On display in rooms that have stood since 1757 are items once used by the house's original builders and owners. Should one be fortunate enough, one might even catch a glimpse of the spirit known only as Elizabeth.

Bishop Huntington House has been known as Forty Acres, Porter Mansion, Phelps Mansion and Huntington Mansion. Its resident ghost has only been known by one name since she first began to make her presence known— Elizabeth. Her exact identity remains a mystery, since three generations of Elizabeths all lived in the house. Most believe Elizabeth is the spirit of Bishop Huntington House's first Elizabeth. Hers, after all, is a saga of grief and loss—

Elizabeth is the spiritual occupant of Bishop Huntington House in Hadley, Massachusetts.

the sort of tragedy that seems to be the basis for many hauntings.

The first marriage to take place in Hadley joined Aaron Cooke and Sarah Westwood. Seeking to advance their daughter's social position, the couple arranged for her to be married to Samuel Porter, Jr., who had the distinction of being the first male born in Hadley, as well as the scion of one of the most powerful families in the flourishing community.

Porter's father had made his fortune in alcohol and owned one of only two stills in the county. There was no shortage of customers looking to end a hard day's work farming in the fields with a little of what they called Demon Rum. The resulting profits allowed Porter to acquire huge swaths of land, most of it north of Hadley proper. Grandson Moses Porter brought his wife, Elizabeth, to live there when he built the first home on the land. It was a simple two-story affair crowned with a peaked roof. It boasted (and still boasts) two cooking fireplaces and a smoke oven. To mark the home's completion and to honor his family, Porter planted three American elm trees in the yard—one for his daughter, Betty, another for his wife and the last for himself. Of the three, one has survived two centuries of inclement weather, much as the spirit of Bishop Huntington House has.

The Porter family spent three happy years in their home until their bliss was shattered by the first skirmishes of the French–Indian Wars. Porter had worked far too long and hard on his land—as his father had before him—to lose it all to the French and their Indian allies. He joined the Massachusetts militia and took up arms in the names of Britain, King George II and God to drive the French from North America. On the morning of September 8, 1755, Porter and a company of men were ambushed by an Indian war party near the southern end of Lake George in New York. Most of the men were massacred in what became known as the Battle of the Bloody Morning Scout. Porter was among those who lay dead.

Meanwhile, back at the house Elizabeth was tucking their daughter into bed for the night. She stroked Betty's hair, all the while singing a lullaby. The melody finished, she kissed her sweet child on the forehead and wished her a good night. It was the last thing she ever did with any semblance of normalcy.

The next moment, Elizabeth's life changed forever. There was a knock on the window. Elizabeth slid open the shutters and saw her husband's Indian servant standing in front of her, his face creased with grief and dark with anger. Without a word, he held up his outstretched hands. Lying flat across both palms was a sword in its scabbard. Its hilt winked in the moonlight. Elizabeth immediately knew that her husband was dead. She accepted the sword with a tear and turned to tell her 7-year-old child that she would never see her father again. It's said that both never fully recovered from their grief. That sword can still be seen in the house in the same room where it was received by Porter's widow.

Betty, meanwhile, married Charles Phelps in 1779 and gave birth to a daughter, another Elizabeth. Elizabeth Whiting Phelps' portrait hangs in the living room to this day. The youngest of her 11 children, Frederic, became the Bishop of Central New York. The house that bears his name today became his summer home.

As generations of Porters passed in and out of the house's halls, they could take great comfort that their ancestors were never far from them. The first Elizabeth was fond of using her spinning wheel in the attic. After her death, the wheel was moved into the kitchen, yet her descendants could still hear her working away in the attic. Also of great comfort was how she would steal into children's rooms at night and tuck them into their beds. Dr. James Huntington, a direct descendant of Moses Porter, recalls waking at night "to find a figure bending over the bed, someone whose full skirt of oddly patterned design and frilled white were perfectly visible in the dark."

Dr. Huntington's brother had his bedroom in the attic and for two nights was frightened out of sleep when he heard someone walking up and down the stairs. In the morning, the door to the attic staircase, locked and secured the night before, was standing wide open. The third night it happened, Dr. Huntington's brother could stand it no longer and fled down the steps where he passed a spirit that looked like a child.

There is another ghost in Bishop Huntington House. It can often be seen napping in the bed that Betty once slept in, although all one really sees is an indentation in the sheets. Straightening them out accomplishes nothing. Within moments, the pillow is deeply indented once more, while the blankets become creased under the weight of a small body. Few are able to determine who this spirit was in life, but researchers have speculated that it may very well be Betty Porter, who spends her afterlife mourning the loss of a father she barely knew, but whose touch, kiss and voice she could never forget. The museum, created by a foundation of the Huntington brothers, ensures that the town of Hadley will remember too,

Ladd House
CHARLESTON, SOUTH CAROLINA

Hindsight offers people another perspective, a chance to reflect upon their actions. At times, great regret inspires people to wonder why they might have said the things they said or done the things they did. If they are fortunate, they learn how their anger and pride can fuel the most innocuous of problems, bloating them until they are conflicts too unwieldy to bear. Hopefully, reconciliation is not far off. Of course, there was a time when even the most insipid of arguments could lead to unavoidable tragedy. In Charleston, South Carolina, Ladd House stands as a not-so-silent testament to a different era—a time when the slightest provocation or insult to a man's honor meant an invitation to "judicial combat" or what was more commonly known as a duel.

Imported from Europe, dueling was a means of defending honor under the eyes of God. God would judge the combatants and let the one in the right win. Its importance in the South, where old-fashioned chivalry once prevailed, cannot be understated. Those who refused a challenge were named in newspapers or on notices posted in public areas and branded cowards. And while there were those who condemned the practice as little more than sanctioned murder, dueling was still regarded as a means of avoiding violence and mending grievances. How else could one possibly explain why, in 1786, a part-time doctor and poet, Joseph Brown Ladd, marched onto the dueling grounds of Charleston to face Ralph Isaacs, with whom he had been in an argument over the talents of a young Shakespearean actress?

The ghost of Joseph Brown Ladd haunts his former home—a result, no doubt, of his tragic demise after an 18th-century duel.

Ladd was a doctor and a poet. On the advice of General Nathanael Greene, he traveled to Charleston from Rhode Island in 1784 to open a practice. While there, he was successful and continued to write, inspired often by the woman he considered his greatest muse, an orphan heiress named Amanda. Theirs was a love that was doomed from the start. Despite the couple's desire to be together, Amanda's guardians refused to allow it. It seemed that they were far from scrupulous, and her estate was far more valuable to them if she were single.

The young lovers conceived a plan. He would leave Rhode Island and settle in South Carolina. After establishing his practice, he would send for her. There, far from the meddlesome hands of her guardians, they would be joined forever. He promised her as much in his poem *Absence*, undeniably a lament, but one graced with hope for a future where "blest in meeting, both shall live." But where Amanda's guardians had failed, fate would succeed.

According to Margaret Rhett Martin in *Charleston Ghosts*, Ladd is believed to have met the man who would kill him the moment he arrived in South Carolina. Ralph Isaacs saved the young doctor from harm that first day in Charleston. Ladd had run into a gang of young hoodlums bent on theft and perhaps more. Isaacs intervened, running the lawless characters off. With such an introduction, it's no surprise that Ladd and Isaacs quickly become the closest of friends. Unfortunately, as would soon become clear, Isaacs was a petty man.

Ladd was blessed with gifts that had been denied Isaacs. Where Isaacs struggled to find his place in society, the same society was eager to make a place for Ladd, the young doctor with the soul of a poet. Charleston clamored for Ladd's attention, aching to gaze upon his handsome visage, to be swayed by his ample charms and to revel in his intelligence. As Ladd's popularity grew, Isaacs felt as if he were being pushed farther and farther into the shadows, his moon eclipsed by the brilliance of the sun. He longed to spend more time with Ladd but Ladd's social calendar grew ever busier by the day.

One evening, the two took in a play at the local theater. Isaacs' resentment had fomented a raging jealousy and madness took hold. When Ladd offered a different assessment of the lead actress' performance, Isaacs could not contain himself, initiating an argument that led to the dissolution of their friendship. The argument escalated into a war of words in which both parties traded barbs and insults in the *Charleston Gazette*. To Isaacs, Ladd was "as blasted a scoundrel as ever disgraced humanity." The damage to Ladd's reputation was immediate and, fearful as to what harm it might do to his plans with Amanda, he consulted friends for advice.

His friends, being 18th-century gentlemen, stated that a duel was the only way. Ladd reluctantly challenged his old friend. It may have been what Isaacs had been hoping for all along. On October 12, 1786, Ladd walked out to the dueling grounds. He was unsure about the whole affair. The challenge had been made halfheartedly and the absurdity of the situation flustered him. He was a doctor, trained to heal, not to kill. He longed to apologize, to satisfy Isaacs' honor, but to do so meant risking additional damage to his already flagging reputation. Being pilloried in public as a coward would not help bring Amanda to Charleston. The die had been cast and Ladd had already crossed the Rubicon.

Standing back-to-back with Isaacs, Ladd made the decision that when they had marched their ten paces and turned to fire, he would not shoot. Instead, he would fire his pistol harmlessly into the air and prayed that God would help Isaacs to realize the pointlessness of their conflict. Of course, Ladd did not perceive the extent to which Isaacs' envy had consumed him. If he had, Ladd would have been very scared indeed.

Ladd fired his shot carefully into the air, according to his plan. But Isaacs was bent on destroying the precious doctor. He didn't want only to kill the man, since death seemed too easy a fate. He wanted Ladd to suffer as he had suffered, to fade into obscurity. Ladd would watch as former friends and acquaintances shied away from the man who had lost the duel to Isaacs, who had been judged wrong by God Himself. Isaacs, seeing that Ladd had fired into the air, pressed his advantage. He shot Ladd twice, once beneath each knee. Ladd would be a cripple. Such was the terrible power of envy.

Ladd was rushed to the house he rented from Fannie and Dellie Rose at 59 Church Street. If he did survive, he would be crippled, but surgeons feared much worse. Gangrene poisoning had affected both knees, and there was little else doctors could do. Ladd lingered in bed for three weeks, increasingly aware of his own mortality. He asked for only one thing: to see Amanda one last time. The Roses sent urgent messages to Rhode Island pleading for Amanda's presence. Her guardians, however, would not permit it; she was watched day and night to prevent her escape. On November 2, Ladd took his final breath. He had spent his last days feverish and delirious. Lucid moments were few, but when they came all Ladd would whisper was "Amanda."

Since his death, rumors persist that Ladd never left the house he had rented at 59 Church Street. He enters with a blast of cold air, as if he had just walked through a door. His footsteps are heard soon after, creaking their way up the staircase. At the top of the landing, the whistled melody of an old English ballad fills the darkened hallways. But not everyone is convinced.

As told in an article Susan Hill Smith wrote in 1998, Cathy Forrester has lived at the house since 1988, when her grandparents, who had bought the home in 1941, passed away. She told Smith that she's a "ghost skeptic" yet still admits to having seen something unusual in the house when she first moved in.

"Out of the corner of my eye," Forrester told Smith, "I thought I saw a figure on the landing. It was a man, not dressed in contemporary clothes. It was just a split-second thing."

Forrester also described events that her grandmother, Juliette Staats, had recalled. Overnight guests often slept in the second-floor guest bedroom where Ladd is believed to have died. As it is in so many other haunted houses, these unfortunate guests find sleep elusive, largely on account of someone walking the staircase during the night. One guest woke up one evening with a start and wrote three letters down on a sheet of paper: JBL. He showed the letters to Staats and asked her if they were significant. She smiled, recognizing them as John Brown Ladd's monogram. But despite this event and others involving unexplained noises, Staats, like her granddaughter, remained skeptical. Smith reports that on the *Today* show in 1986, Staats, when asked if she believed in ghosts, answered, "If I believed in ghosts, I would believe he was a very good friend of the house and sort of protects the house and everyone who's in it."

Of course, even if they mean to protect the house, there are those who still would rather not have anything to do with the spirits of the dead. Andrew Frost believed in ghosts but wanted nothing to do with them. He worked the house for over 20 years, cleaning and doing odd jobs. Renovators who once worked the home got used to Frost coming around until they realized that the man they took for Frost wasn't really Frost at all, but Ladd's ghost.

Frost lost his patience with the spirit that constantly walked the halls and slammed the doors on the second and third floors. Smith writes that when it first happened, he thought it might have been the cook, but then realized that she was on the first floor with him. As he spent more time in the house, Frost became more and more frustrated and eventually yelled out, "Damn you dead!" Ever since, Frost has worked at the house free of interruption.

But while Frost is free of the ghost, the house is not. Known officially as the Thomas Rose House, in honor of the man who first built the home in 1732, the white-stucco home has acquired an unofficial name recognizing its most famous and tragic inhabitant. Ladd House is still home to the ghost of a man who wanted nothing more in life than to love his Amanda but could not. Pride crippled him, leading him to the duel that took his life. In hindsight, when weighed against life, a man's reputation and honor may not be the most precious of things.

Ringwood Manor
SADDLE RIVER, NEW JERSEY

Ringwood has always been a popular place. Even before the first European settlers arrived to mine the rich iron deposits, Native American tribes hunted and fished in the area, staying in the Ringwood area for months at a time at the head of the Ringwood River Valley. One tribe in particular, the Lenapi, revered the location, believing it to be an area especially prone to supernatural occurrences and natural earth forces.

European settlers coveted the valleys for their wealth in natural resources. Under the surface, exerting the magnetic force that the Lenapi felt so strongly, were veins of magnetite iron ore. But while the land aroused awe in the Lenapi, it fed avarice in the Europeans. In the stands of chestnut, hickory, elm and oak, the Europeans saw charcoal. In the waters that drained through the valley in rapid streams, the Europeans saw the power necessary to run their mills and machinery. In the veins of iron, the Europeans saw smelting. But as the veins were depleted through the years and the iron industry migrated away from New Jersey, Ringwood's economic prominence faded. Once again, Ringwood is a supernatural land, a place where all that remains of its once mighty iron industry is a 51-room mansion haunted by a host of spirits.

The Europeans first began displacing Native American tribes from the bucolic splendor of the Ringwood River valley in 1740 when Cornelius Board first discovered that the valley basin offered veins of iron that descended for thousands of feet. But Board's operation remained small, paling in comparison to that of the Ogden family who

Ghostly former occupants of Ringwood Manor in New Jersey react differently to renovations to the property.

followed Board's lead. In 1742, Ogden, newly arrived from Hampshire County, England, built his first furnace to become the first large-volume producer of iron in New Jersey. He christened his new venture the Ringwood Company, bestowing upon the area the name by which it would forever be known.

Ringwood Manor began as a humble structure that was slightly enlarged in 1762 when profits from the Ringwood

Company allowed Ogden to do so. The mansion didn't truly begin to take shape until the American Revolution, when George Washington's cartographer, Robert Erskine, made Ringwood his headquarters for three iron-making plantations. A patriot, Erskine drew up over 200 highly detailed and accurate maps for the colonial army, and Washington himself paid numerous visits to Ringwood. After the death of the Erskines, the haunting of Ringwood began.

Martin J. Ryerson was the next owner of the home. He continued to prosper in the lucrative iron industry, creating the Ryerson Steel Company, a business that still runs today. In 1807, he tore down the home that Ogden had first erected and rebuilt it completely. The changes did not sit well with certain parties, notably Mrs. Erskine. The majority of the hauntings in Ringwood take place in what was once Mrs. Erskine's bedroom, before it was torn down to suit Ryerson's needs. And even though she had died years before, Mrs. Erskine returned to Ringwood to voice her displeasure, which she is believed to do through opening locked doors and creating cold spots.

Ryerson found his new home almost more trouble than it was worth. Every night, he would make sure that all the doors and windows were locked shut; every morning, he would awaken only to find that all the doors and windows were wide open. The only spirit that could keep Mrs. Erskine in check was that of Jeremiah, a disgruntled former servant of Mrs. Erskine who accused his mistress of mistreating him and had now returned to keep his former employer in line. While Mrs. Erskine remained to haunt the living, Jeremiah was there only to haunt the woman who had tormented him so mercilessly in life. Despite the problems in his new home, Ryerson soon found himself with far more pressing matters.

By the 1830s, the iron industry was stagnating. Veins were exhausted and companies were abandoning the northeast for richer veins in the west. In order to save his dwindling fortune, Ryerson sold the property to wealthy inventor and industrialist Peter Cooper and his son-in-law, Abram S. Hewitt, in 1854. Hewitt had made his fortunes running smelting operations throughout the northeastern states and bought Ringwood with an eye on transforming the 38,000 acres on which the complex sat into an exquisite summer estate.

Mrs. Hewitt, inspired by tours throughout Europe's castles, initiated changes in the mansion that gave the home its grand but slightly off-kilter look. The renovations incorporated a curious blend of Dutch, Tudor and Italian influences and meshed four buildings into one with 51 rooms, 24 fireplaces, 13 bathrooms, 28 bedrooms and more than 250 windows. It was the perfect retreat for the Hewitt family and an appropriate look for what would become known as the Second White House.

Hewitt may have once been interested in the iron industry, but his business now was politics; he used his wealth and the influence it afforded him to become chairman of the Democratic National Committee. While her husband set about trying to run the country, Hewitt's wife Sarah set about dismantling the forges, mills and farms that had been used in the iron industry, and did her best to return the land its original pristine state. Sarah considered herself a landscape artist and replaced the rotting, rusting remains of the forges with ponds, shrubs and trees. She is best remembered for the creation of Sarah's Pond, essentially a miniature lake used to reflect the glory of the Ringwood Manor in its entirety.

This addition appears to have pleased Mr. Erskine. Upon his death, Erskine was buried in a cemetery on the property, one that also held the interred bodies of more than 400 pioneers, early ironmakers, Revolutionary War soldiers and even French soldiers. The completion of the pond must have restored his spirits; he has been known to rise from his grave, perch upon his headstone and stare wistfully out across the pond, often taking people walking along its shores by surprise.

Erskine is not the only ghost who enjoys Sarah's Pond. Another apparition occasionally appears, although she prefers to enjoy the pond's splendor alone. Her identity is unknown, but she chases away those who intrude upon her solitude. Fishermen have had their rods and tackle boxes disappear from their sides, only to reappear mysteriously in their vehicles later. Perhaps the woman is Sarah Hewitt, who is known to haunt the mansion's interior, or that of Mrs. Erskine, who has apparently told ghost researchers through a medium that she wants to leave and get off her property.

The Hewitts prospered at Ringwood, but their offspring chose a different path than their forebears. Instead of pursuing politics or the iron industry, the next generation of Hewitts decided that the great estate was simply too much. The iron industry was faltering and it was clear that while the Hewitts had been one of the most influential and powerful families, the sun was setting on their empire. But the Hewitts did not want to see everything that their father had worked for torn asunder, so Ringwood—the manor and the grounds—were given to the state of New Jersey. In so doing, the grand estate was placed on the National Register of Historic Places, although its acreage has been vastly trimmed. Instead of spanning 38,000 acres, the grounds now cover 582. The mansion, transformed into a museum, is as stunning and regal as it was in Sarah Hewitt's day and, by all accounts, just as haunted.

Footsteps echo throughout the museums, even when it is supposedly empty. Curators and museum staff swear that there are at least two distinct ghosts walking through the home. One is believed to be Erskine, while the second might be a man named Jackson White, a descendant of runaway slaves who had settled in the Ringwood Valley during the Civil War. Both are known to frequent the upstairs and downstairs corridors; visitors walking through them sometimes hear voices and often find themselves subjected to cold spots. The voices sometimes speak French, leading one to believe that perhaps some soldiers have come in from the cold to take refuge in the elaborate confines of the Ringwood home.

The last iron mine in Ringwood closed down in the 1950s. By that time, the glory of the Hewitt family and those who had preceded them at Ringwood could only be revisited in memory. Of course, its reality can be experienced and touched through a trip to the Ringwood Manor, where the past comes to life in ways few could anticipate. People still come to Ringwood, although it's not for iron these days. Like the ancient and long-forgotten Lenapi, people come to Ringwood now because it occupies a place in their consciousness. Ringwood has become hallowed ground—a place where the lines between the living and the dead are blurred, where history breathes and moves with a vitality all its own.

Dickinson Mansion
DOVER, DELAWARE

There is an old English ballad that proclaims that a woman's work is never done, that "no man can imagine what a woman must do." Yet in the case of lawyer John Dickinson, it's a man's work that is never done. For even after the so-called "Penman of the Revolution" died in 1808, his ghost still returns to the house in which he wrote so many of the essays on colonial rights and liberty for which he was known. Inside the home that bears his name, Dickinson continues to work diligently, displaying the same temper, discipline and dedication that won him the respect of so many admirers as he labored at the Constitutional Convention.

John Dickinson arrived in Dover, Delaware, as an 8-year-old boy. His father, a wealthy Quaker tobacco planter, had accepted a judgeship there that would allow his wife Mary to be closer to her family in Philadelphia. They settled on a plantation called Poplar Hall where John was rigorously schooled by his parents and a succession of tutors. As it did to his father before him, law beckoned the young Dickinson and it wasn't long before he was studying the profession in Philadelphia. Gifted and able, Dickinson honed his skills in the courts of England, in Middle Temple and Westminster. When he returned to Pennsylvania, it was with a newfound confidence that had been lacking previously in the young man's temperament. His superior oratory skills and keen political instincts took him to the Pennsylvania legislature. From there, Dickinson waged a campaign against the British government and the liberties they were taking with the

Paranormal research seems to indicate that the Revolutionary War politician John Dickinson hasn't stopped penning documents.

colonials. The colonials, in turn, embraced the man who gave them a genuine voice, one quite unlike anything they had ever had.

But unlike other politicians of the time, Dickinson preached compromise and refused to believe that a declaration of independence was the wisest of decisions. And so, while he had been chosen by the state of Pennsylvania to be its representative at the first Congress in New York, his resistance towards independence nearly crippled his political career. As it was, his unpopularity was so overwhelming that he was forced to abandon politics for two years. He eventually returned to favor, finding success as governor of Delaware and president of the Supreme Executive Council of Pennsylvania. While he never supported complete independence from Great Britain, Dickinson is still considered one of the greatest patriots, a man who believed in the rule of law but not at the expense of individual freedoms, and whose integrity never wavered or yielded. He died in 1808, having spent the last few years of his life in the pursuit of literature and philanthropy. But not even death could keep the good patriot at bay. Dickinson has returned to the mansion that now bears his name, where visitors can immerse themselves in history. While the mansion's architecture bears the unmistakable print of both Samuel Dickinson and his son, the home carries within it the spirit of the latter.

Staff working at the historic site often left the house scratching their heads, wondering what was wrong with the bed in Dickinson's old bedroom. No matter how tightly the sheets were tucked or the blankets were pulled, the bed refused to stay made. Over the course of a day, staff might make and remake the bed to the point where their efforts seemed utterly futile. Something or someone was taking naps in the bedroom, and the slumbering form made deep indentations in the pillow and comforter.

Determined to uncover the identity of the spirit, researchers left a tape recorder running in rooms throughout the house, hoping to capture sounds that the ear alone can't pick up. Most of the recordings captured nothing but typical background noise, but on one, taken in the den where Dickinson

The haunted Dickinson mansion in Dover, Delaware

is said to have written most of his work, there was an unfamiliar scratching sound. When a historical interpreter heard the tape, he said it sounded just as if someone was writing with a quill pen on parchment. Could it be Dickinson writing from beyond the grave? Many people believe it is.

The Dickinson mansion stood for over 250 years, while the museum has been open since 1956. It sits on an 18-acre site along the St. Jones River that includes the 1740 colonial brick home and a number of reconstructed buildings uncovered during archaeological excavations. Throughout the museum, period guides interpret and reenact life as it was in the late 18th century. But no guide could bring the past to life as ably and tangibly as the late John Dickinson who still calls Dickinson mansion home.

House in the Horseshoe
CENTRAL NORTH CAROLINA

At one point in northern Moore County, the Deep River bends and curves sharply, forming what the locals fondly refer to as the horseshoe. Overlooking the bend is a hill, upon which sits a mansion. Once the center of a grand plantation, the property is believed to be the first of the uplands big houses in North Carolina frontier country. The house once anchored a plantation that sprawled over 7000 acres and was home to one of the more vibrant characters in the state's history, Philip Alston. Fittingly enough, Alston still calls the House in the Horseshoe home. Ever since the first of a long series of unexplained events took place in the house, Alston's movements have given the living something to talk about for years now.

Alston arrived in Moore County in 1772. A son of wealth and influence, Alston wanted for little, and even though his inheritance had been far less than expected, Alston had no need of his father's fortune. With his own sizable wealth he bought 4000 acres of land north and south of the horseshoe in Deep River. His house was intended to make a grand statement.

Hiring a Scotsman named McFadden, Alston had a mansion built on a hill overlooking the Deep River. Upon its completion, it was hailed as one of the finest homes in all the Carolinas. Only the finest of the local social elite passed through its doorways. But the idyll didn't last long. When shots were fired at British soldiers in 1775 at Lexington and Concord, the colonies entered war with their former master. Some felt that confrontation with Britain was something to be avoided, that a compromise would be a better solution. One such man was Colonel David Fanning.

One evening, while escorting rebel prisoners to Wilmington, Fanning decided to pay a visit to the house of friend, Kenneth Black. After he spent the night there, Black gave Fanning his fresh steed the next morning to replace Fanning's lame beast of burden. Later Black came upon a platoon of colonial soldiers who recognized him as a monarchist. At the command of their superior, one Philip Alston, the colonials launched into a pursuit of Black. Black never got far; with his lame horse, it was easy for a skilled marksman to shoot the desperate Black off his mount. Alston dismounted and walked over to Black, who lay wounded and trapped under his horse. He begged to be spared, told Alston about the family he had waiting at home for him, about his children who shouldn't be deprived of their father. Alston wouldn't hear any of it. It was war, he reasoned, and the enemy was the enemy. Drawing Black's pistol from its holster, Alston held it by its butt and then beat Black to death.

When Fanning learned what had happened, he rode out to Alston's house. While surprise was on his side, he quickly lost the advantage; the two sides eventually fought themselves to a standstill. Indeed, Fanning was ready to signal a retreat. Scouts had told him of an advancing party of colonials against which Fanning's small group would have had little hope of defeating.

But just then Fanning spotted an oxcart in the yard. A wicked plan formed in his mind. He directed his men to fill the cart with hay, set it on fire and ram the cart through Alston's front door. If they stayed in the house, they would burn. If they fled, Fanning's men would shoot them dead. The plan was beautiful and terrible in its simplicity. Yet Fanning stayed his hand. A white flag had presented itself at the door and despite his longing for revenge for Black's death, he was still a gentleman. He signaled his men to stop filling the cart and called for the person bearing the white flag to come speak with him.

A woman appeared from behind the door, a person Fanning recognized as Mrs. Alston. The men sent her out because they feared that they would be shot as soon as they showed themselves. Mrs. Alston pleaded with her tormentor. She so impressed him with her courage and wisdom that Fanning agreed to spare her husband and his men. But while a narrow escape from death is often sufficient to change a man, Alston remained as reckless and cruel as he had always been.

At the conclusion of the Revolutionary War, Alston became a member of the state senate. He may have gained political power, but he failed to realize that there are always some who seek to topple the influential from their perches. Not surprisingly, it was his past that threatened to unseat Alston. Evidence was presented supporting the case that Alston had murdered a Thomas Taylor during the war as commander of a corps of militia. Only a pardon from Governor Caswell and Alston's assertion that the man's death was a legitimate act of war saved his political career. But the damage had been done.

Doubt had been introduced into the minds of those he meant to serve. When George Glascock challenged Alston's seat on the General Assembly, all he had to do to gain the public's favor was remind them of Alston's questionable past and his lack of belief in God. Alston was dismissed from office.

Months later, Glascock met a suspicious death at the hands of one of Alston's slaves. Investigators attempting to implicate Alston in the crime were thwarted; Alston had spent the evening of Glascock's murder entertaining guests in his lavish plantation home. Alston posted bail for his slave and when the slave escaped and did not appear for his trial, very few people were surprised. The judges were not among them.

Alston was fined for contempt of court and sentenced to time in Wilmington Jail. He escaped confinement and fled North Carolina in disgrace. He was found murdered in Georgia in 1791, shot as he lay sleeping. Rumors suggest that it was his slave who shot him. His family, shamed and embarrassed, sold Alston's property for what they could and left North Carolina. But while they left, Alston is believed to have returned. He found a home markedly different from the one he had left behind.

In 1798, Governor Benjamin Williams moved onto the plantation and enlarged the mansion, adding two wings, a kitchen and another master bedroom. In the land he saw potential for vast profit and began raising cotton, a task made much easier with the invention of Eli Whitney's cotton gin. He died a wealthy man in 1814. His descendants lived in the house until 1853, after which time the house changed ownership again and again until the state bought it in 1955. Since then, it has served as a North Carolina State historic site, host to a yearly reenactment of the engagement between

Unexplained paranormal phenomena recur at the House in the Horseshoe in central North Carolina.

Alston and Fanning. Upon close inspection, bullet holes from the conflict can still be seen, as well as a much more mysterious remnant.

On nights when the air is still and the moon is full, individuals passing Alston House have been startled to see the historic site become the center of some highly irregular activity. Accounts describe a strange light moving quickly across the ground before soaring high into the air, arcing its way across the starlit sky. Inside the home, tours are often supplemented not only by knowledgeable interpreters, but also by assistance from beyond. Phantom footsteps can sometimes be a point of interest on the tour, as can the whispers that come from the fireplace and the high-pitched squealing that tears through the house. Although no one can say for certain who is behind the unusual happenings, most point to Philip Alston. With such a will and personality, it's not unreasonable to assume that death failed to keep the colonel in check. It was in the very same house, after all, that he escaped certain death through his wife's fortunate intervention. Perhaps Alston has found a new lease on life in the afterlife. Regardless, a visit to his former home would surely be a good starting point for a journey into an entirely different world.

Castle Hill Mansion
CASTLE HILL, VIRGINIA

Dr. Thomas Walker rose out of his bed. The knocking at his front door was loud and insistent, and whoever was at the door gave no sign of relenting. Walker should have been upset, but he wasn't. It was a time of war and colonials had often come to his house on Castle Hill in Virginia to seek shelter or supplies.

He wearily got out of bed, calling out to the unknown visitor that he was on his way. With lit lantern, he opened the door and drew back in fear. Standing before him, wreathed in the flickering shadows of candlelight, was a giant man. His eyes were wild with desperation and his face was bloody.

Walker soon learned that the man was Jack Jouett, a captain in the Virginia militia. Jouett's mission might prove decisive in the war for freedom. He had already traveled 40 miles through thick trees whose branches had torn at his face. His horse was nearly dead with exhaustion. Jouett asked Dr. Walker for a fresh mount so that he might speed his journey to Monticello. He needed to get word to Thomas Jefferson and 40 members of the legislature to flee the city ahead of the advancing British, who were closing in fast under the command of Colonel Banastre Tarleton and his force of 180 dragoons and 70 mounted infantrymen. As he mounted a fresh steed, he asked the doctor for one more favor. Walker watched Jouett expectantly.

"If they stop here," Jouett instructed, "delay them. Delay them for as long as you can. My journey depends upon it."

Dr. Walker gave his word and watched Jouett disappear into the darkness. He then rushed into his home, woke his wife and began to make preparations for the soldiers' arrival.

Tarleton and his men arrived a short time later, just as the rosy tendrils of the morning sun were creeping across the horizon. Tarleton dismounted and demanded that Dr. Walker provide him and his men with food.

Dr. Walker and his wife welcomed the redcoats into their home. Their cook had already been warned to delay the preparation of the soldiers' meals for as long as possible. While the men waited, the Walkers served the men round upon round of heavily spiked mint juleps, hoping to dull their senses. The ruse worked, if only for a short while. Although Tarleton was slightly inebriated, he was not unobservant. He stormed into the kitchen, demanding to know why the food was so long in coming. The cooks pleaded ignorance. Tarleton slammed a fist on a table demanding no more delays and then turned abruptly to leave the kitchen.

The food was served and the men soon made ready to ride again. Walker tried to delay, offering them more food and asking them if they would like to rest for a little while longer. Tarleton politely, but firmly, refused all such entreaties. Dr. Walker's wife then approached the colonel.

"Colonel," she said, "your road is long and it is hard. You have already traveled so far and to such lengths. Surely there must be something else here that you want. The constant company of men, here in a strange and foreign land, could not possibly be fulfilling."

Tarleton paused, asking his men to halt. It had been far too long since he had experienced the soft and delicate touch of a woman. Months had passed since he had last buried his face in a woman's tresses.

"We will stay here a while longer."

Hours passed before the colonel emerged from the house. The men were ordered to move and he followed, saluting the good doctor and his wife and thanked them for their hospitality.

The Walkers learned to their great relief later that Jouett had managed to reach Monticello with his message. Jefferson and the 40 members of legislature—among them Patrick Henry, Thomas Lee and Benjamin Harrison—had fled the city, spiriting away Tarleton's prize. Jouett's ride, Dr. Walker's manipulation and his wife's offer had saved Thomas Jefferson from capture. And while Jouett and Walker departed this earth long ago, the house on Castle Hill remains, standing as testament to their courage. And so too does Walker's wife.

Walker built the stately residence in 1764, inviting such luminaries as James Madison and Thomas Jefferson to grace its halls. The wooden structure he erected, however, proved susceptible to erosion. In 1823, owner William Cabel Rives, a U.S. senator and Confederate congressman, used brick to augment and bolster the sagging wooden frames. Rives was decadent and the home reflects his tastes. Brick was imported from England, glass and other fixtures came from London. He erected a row of Doric columns to run the length of the house.

While Rives lived there, he never experienced anything out of the ordinary. It wasn't until his granddaughter, novelist Amelie Rives, had taken possession of the house that Castle Hill's haunted history can be said to begin. Married to Russian painter Pierre Troubetzkoy, Rives was a prominent social figure who enjoyed entertaining guests, friends and members of the social elite. Overnight guests, common at Castle Hill, were the first to experience phenomena they could not explain.

Over breakfast, guests would complain to their hosts about how they were unable to sleep. Many had been kept awake all night by the constant ascent and descent of the staircase by unseen figures. Voices, loud enough to raise the dead (ironically enough, it was probably the dead who were speaking), woke others from sleep. Yet when the perturbed guests left their rooms to investigate the conversations they heard just outside their doors, there was no one to be found.

Amelie herself was constantly enveloped by clouds of a perfume, the likes of which she had never worn. Guests would ask her where she bought such beautiful rose-scented water, and Amelie would then know that Castle Hill's permanent resident had a paid a visit.

As the years passed, the ghost grew bolder. A former housekeeper at the house described how someone would grab her leg any time she slept without covers. And guests staying in what would become known as the pink bedroom reported frequent disturbances throughout the evening, all at the hands of a young pretty woman who was alternately playful and frightening. Strangely though, there were guests who slept in the pink bedroom without interruption. The belief is that the pretty young ghost is selective with the people she chooses to disturb. Should you strike her fancy, your stay will be one of blissful ease.

Writer Julian Green, a skeptic who denied the existence of ghosts, stayed in the pink bedroom one evening. He fled the home sometime during the evening without even bidding farewell to his hosts. He never discussed what had happened. The reasons for his sudden departure accompanied Green to his grave when he died in 1998. Of course one can hazard a guess as to what happened. After all, Green was not the only visitor to flee Castle Hill. One guest described how a beautiful woman, dressed in clothing dating back almost two centuries, had awakened him and then whispered in his ear that he had to go, that he could not stay. The incident fully unnerved the man, and whenever he was asked to discuss his experience, he became incoherent and shook his arms in the air. Apparently, Green was one of those of whom the ghost didn't approve.

No one is sure who this female ghost is, but she appears to have the final say in who gets to sleep in what must have once been her bedroom. Some speculate that the pretty apparition is the reincarnation of Dr. Walker's wife. Her clothing appears to match the fashions of the late 18th century, and as one of the house's original tenants, she may believe that she still has the authority to decide who is allowed to stay at her house. Why not? It is her right. Without her, Colonel Tarleton might have succeeded in his quest to capture Thomas Jefferson and bring the colonials to their knees.

THE END

Enjoy more haunting tales in these collections by

GHOST HOUSE

GHOST HOUSE BOOKS

The colorful history of North America includes many spine-tingling tales of the supernatural. These fun, fascinating books by GHOST HOUSE BOOKS reveal the rich diversity of haunted places on the continent and beyond. Our ghostly tales involve well-known theaters, buildings and other landmarks, many of which are still in use. Watch for these new titles!

Haunted Highways *by Dan Asfar*
Lights on the road. Ghost hitchhikers. Eerie covered bridges. Dan Asfar shows how some of America's most innocuous streets and thoroughfares can suddenly become terrifying haunts.
$10.95US/$14.95CDN   ISBN 1-894877-29-2   5.25" x 8.25"   224 pages

Haunted Schools *by A.S. Mott*
Schools are centers of learning, respected for their rational approach to the world we live in. But many of North America's schools are also hotbeds of the unexplained, where ghosts terrify the living with lessons they won't forget.
$10.95US/$14.95CDN   ISBN 1-894877-32-2   5.25" x 8.25"   232 pages

Ghost Stories of the Old South *by Edrick Thay*
The Old South is one of America's most mysterious regions. In this exciting new collection, you'll explore centers of paranormal lore, such as Savannah and Charleston, and learn about stubborn ghosts obsessed with the survival of Old Dixie.
$10.95US/$14.95CDN   ISBN 1-894877-18-7   5.25" x 8.25"   232 pages

Ghost Stories of the Old West *by Dan Asfar*
The OK Corral, Fort Leavenworth, Billy the Kid, the Pony Express—the old West had it all. Join Dan Asfar as he uncovers the charismatic ghosts who inhabit the prisons, forts and saloons where the West was born—and died.
$10.95US/$14.95CDN   ISBN 1-894877-17-9   5.25" x 8.25"   232 pages

Also look for
Haunted Hotels by Jo-Anne Christensen   ISBN 1-894877-03-9
Haunted Theaters by Barbara Smith   ISBN 1-894877-04-7
Campfire Ghost Stories by Jo-Anne Christensen   ISBN 1-894877-02-0

These and many more *Ghost House* books are available from your local bookseller or by ordering direct. U.S. readers call 1-800-518-3541.
In Canada, call 1-800-661-9017.